Unique Evidences
OF THE Restoration

E. Keith Howick

Unique Evidences
OF THE Restoration

E. Keith Howick

WindRiver Publishing • Silverton, Idaho

LDS.WindRiverPublishing.com

Unique Evidences of the Restoration
Copyright ©2008 by E. Keith Howick

WindRiver Publishing, the WindRiver Brand Logo, and the WindRiver Windmill Logo are trademarks of WindRiver Publishing, Inc.

Library of Congress Control Number: 2008924030
ISBN-13 978-1-886249-35-6
ISBN-10 1-886249-35-0

Printed in the United States by Malloy, Inc. on acid-free paper

Contents

Section III   Restoring the Church of the Firstborn

Section IV   Doctrinal Evidences

Section V   Judgment and the Kingdoms Of Glory

Section VI   Final Evidences

For the time will come when they will not endure sound doctrine; but after their own lusts shall they heap to themselves teachers, having itching ears; And they shall turn away their ears from the truth, and shall be turned unto fables.

2 Timothy 4:3–4

Preface

The Church of Jesus Christ of Latter-day Saints claims to be the only true church upon the earth today. With the Church's emphasis on missionary work, have you ever wished you had access to information that could not only strengthen your own knowledge, but witness to your friends and neighbors that this claim is true? Many unique and powerful evidences prove that the gospel of Jesus Christ, lost during the Great Apostasy, was, in fact divinely restored by the Prophet Joseph Smith in the latter days.

Many opponents of the LDS Church argue against the Restoration, claiming that the original church Christ established in the meridian of time continued after His crucifixion and after the deaths of His Apostles. The Catholic Church claims a full succession from the original church, and the Protestant churches came into being as they "reformed" the alleged errors of Catholicism. But today, none of these churches, nor any that have broken away from them, satisfy the scriptural requirements of prophecy, doctrine, and organization that existed in Christ's original church. Only the LDS Church meets these criteria.

The purpose of this book is to help members of the Church learn about these restored gospel principles and to teach them to their families, friends, and neighbors; to help them understand that through time, many gospel truths were lost or corrupted, and that a restoration of the gospel in its purity was necessary for mankind to again enjoy life in the Father's kingdom.

To accomplish this goal, this book scripturally identifies twenty-eight unique and distinct evidences of the great latter-day Restoration that *validate* the restoration of the gospel—the most compelling of which reflect the similarity between the restored Church of Jesus Christ of Latter-day Saints and the church the Savior established during His earthly ministry. These evidences prove that after slumbering through the Dark Ages for fifteen hundred years, the gospel of the Prince of Peace has in fact awakened and His church has been delivered "out of the wilderness."

In the dispensation of the fulness of times,
God will gather together in one all things.

Ephesians 1:10

Introduction

The scriptures reveal that historically, the gospel requirements for salvation were given to Adam and his family
soon after the creation. Over time, however, Adam's descendants rejected and/or corrupted the Lord's commandments and fell into apostasy. When the Lord delivered the
children of Israel from bondage, circa 1200 B.C., He restored
the gospel to Moses on Mt. Sinai. But the faithless Israelites rejected it and as a consequence, were given the lesser
Law of Moses.

The Law of Moses was a preliminary law, a schoolmas-
ter to prepare the children of Israel for their coming Messiah.
It foreshadowed Christ's first coming in the meridian of
time, and His mission—the salvation of all mankind. This
was confirmed by all the prophets who lived between the
time the Mosaic Law was given and the Savior's birth.[1]

Israel's long, slow slide into complete apostasy began during the time of the prophet Samuel. Samuel was
a judge in Israel, and perhaps the last prophet to lead a
united Israel under the Law of Moses. Samuel's sons were
not worthy to follow him as prophet and judge, so when
his death appeared imminent, the people approached him

---

1   Galatians 3:24; Malachi 3:1; Matthew 5:17; 11:13; Romans 10:4;
     2 Nephi 25:24-25.

and asked him to appoint a king to govern them. Samuel was distraught. He complained to the Lord that the people had rejected him. But the Lord assured him that the people were not rejecting him as their leader, they were rejecting God as the true Ruler of Israel. So Samuel ordained Saul as the Israelite's first King.[2]

Eventually, the unrighteousness of the Israelites resulted in ten of their tribes being scattered and lost, and by the time Jesus was born a thousand years later, the people were only observing a mere skeleton of the original Law.

When the Lord began His ministry, there were many different sects of Judaism functioning under the Law of Moses: Pharisees, Sadducees, Zealots, Scribes, Essenes, Zodakites, Herodians, Ossaeans, Nasaraeans, Hemerobaptists, and more. The Pharisees (who controlled the synagogues and the schools) and the Sadducees (who controlled the temple and the priestly offices) were the largest of these sects and the ones with which Jesus had the most dealings. But it was this plethora of Jewish sects and their various modes of adhering to the Mosaic Law that caused Jesus to say: "No man putteth a piece of new cloth unto an old garment, for that which is put in to fill it up taketh from the garment, and the rent is made worse. Neither do men put new wine into old bottles: else the bottles break, and the wine runneth out, and the bottles perish . . . ."[3] Because the Jewish leadership was out of step with the Mosaic Law and had fallen away from its spirit and authority, Jesus did not go to them—or to any of the smaller Jewish sects—for assistance in establishing His gospel. In fact, He generally condemned them all for their faithlessness, their pollution of the temple, their worldliness, and their wickedness. They were the "old wine" and "old garments" the Lord was referring to, and were so set in their apostate ways that He could not use them to establish His earthly kingdom.

---

2   1 Samuel 8, 9, 16.

3   Matthew 9:16-17.

But Jesus had come to fulfill the Law of Moses, not to condemn it. He only condemned what the Law had become and the way the Jews were observing it. His mission, therefore, was one of replacement and restoration: replacement of the old Law of Moses with the new law of the gospel, and restoration of the Old Testament prophets' admonitions to live the Law and anticipate the Messiah. Less than four hundred years after the Lord's death, however, the gospel He had established and ultimately given His life for was in complete apostasy. The temple at Jerusalem had been destroyed, there were no apostles to lead the people, revelation had ceased, and the Lord's Spirit was lost as the Dark Ages were ushered in.

To fulfill both Old and New Testament scriptures, the Lord's gospel in its fullness had to be restored before the Second Coming. That restoration occurred through the Prophet Joseph Smith, with the result that the following doctrines challenged those existing in the Christian world, signaling a drastic change from the religious teachings of his day:

- The Lord's church ceased with the deaths of His ancient Apostles.

- The covenant of Abraham was taken from the earth during the Dark Ages.

- God again visits mankind.

- There are more scriptures than one.

- God's authority was lost from the earth.

- A living prophet once again functions upon the earth.

- Revelation from God is once again a reality.

- The call of apostle has been restored to the earth.

- The Lord's gospel includes temples.

- The prophecy in Malachi 4:4–6 has been fulfilled.

None of the Christian churches of Joseph's day either taught or acknowledged these doctrines. And many more doctrines and gospel truths than these would yet be revealed, because the restoration of the Lord's gospel in the latter days would mirror His restoration of the gospel during the meridian of time. And in both instances, His purposes were the same: to fulfill prophecy, to establish His church, and to offer salvation and the opportunity of exaltation to all mankind.

SECTION I

Historical Evidences

Behold, the days come, saith the Lord God,
that I will send a famine in the land, not
a famine of bread, nor a thirst for water,
but of hearing the words of the Lord.

Amos 8:11

The Great Apostasy

For a restoration to occur, there first had to
be a falling away from the Lord's gospel and
from the church He established during His
earthly ministry.

Prior to His ascension, Jesus commissioned His Apostles
to go and "teach all nations, baptizing them in the name
of the Father, and of the Son, and of the Holy Ghost." They
were to teach the people to observe all things that the Lord
had commanded, and He promised them that if they would
do so, He would be with them, "even unto the end of the
world."[1] Bolstered by their witness of the Lord's resurrection and ascension, the Apostles enthusiastically began
fulfilling this commission by preaching salvation in Jerusalem.[2] Since Jesus had declared that He had been sent to
the lost sheep of the house of Israel and not to the world at
large,[3] the Apostles primarily taught the Jews in their syna-

---

1 Matthew 28:19-20; see also Mark 16:15-16.
2 Luke 24:47.
3 Matthew 15:24; Miracles 131.

3

gogues and in their public places.[4] Their initial labors were rewarded with three thousand souls being added to the church.[5] Thus began the formal establishment of Christ's church upon the earth.

"For a time the Church remained completely Jewish, a sect within Israel of those who believed in the resurrection of Jesus and regarded him as the promised Messiah who was about to come again to definitively establish the reign of God."[6] But with the conversion of Cornelius, a Gentile,[7] Peter recognized that the gospel was to be expanded far beyond those of Judah's linage. And Paul, after being aggressively rejected by the Jews in Corinth, shook his raiment and said unto them, "Your blood be upon your own heads; I am clean: from henceforth I will go unto the Gentiles."[8]

The early church spread rapidly, but with growth came dissension, disagreement, and division, causing the early Apostles to prophesy that the

> Christ's ancient church grew rapidly. But with growth came dissension.

fledgling church would not survive. Peter was the first to make this prophecy as he and John chastised the Jews in the temple at Jerusalem for rejecting Christ.

While calling them to repentance, Peter emphasized the fact that Christ had preached to them in the flesh and had been received into heaven. Then he prophesied that the Lord would remain there, "until the times of *restitution* of all things."[9] But to have a "restitution of all things" requires that a falling away must first take place.

As the Apostles preached the gospel throughout the nations bordering the Mediterranean after the Lord's crucifixion, the anticipation of Christ's immediate return in-

---

4   CC 577.

5   Acts 2:41.

6   CHCC 27.

7   Acts 10.

8   Acts 18:6.

9   Acts 3:21. Emphasis added.

creased. Without dampening the spirit generated by the desire to again have the Savior with them, Paul wrote to the Thessalonians and while instructing them concerning Christ's Second Coming, cautioned them to "[b]e not soon shaken in mind, for that day shall not come, except there come a falling away first, and that man of sin [the devil] be revealed."[10] Paul was making it clear to the Thessalonians that the day of Christ's coming was *not* near, and that the Second Coming would not take place until after the devil had caused an apostasy from the truth. He continued to explain that this was a time when Satan with all his delusions would show great "power and signs and lying wonders," and would deceive those who did not love the truth.[11]

True to their prophecies, the falling away began early in the Apostles' ministries. Dissension over doctrine

> The devil caused an apostasy from the truth.

and procedure began almost as rapidly as new converts accepted the gospel. As Gentile converts were brought into the church, the requirements of the Law of Moses and the practice of circumcision became problems. The Jews *knew* they were the chosen people; therefore, they believed that the covenants extended to them under the Law of Moses could not be given to the Gentiles unless the Gentiles also accepted that Law. But Paul saw the gospel as a liberation from the Law, and so argued.[12] This was not the only problem, however. Some of the converts claimed to be Apostles when they were not, and this presented a threat to the authority of the church.[13] Also, some of the Jews who were leaders in the synagogues thought they had authority over the Christian converts, but they were condemned by John the Revelator as being of the "synagogue of Satan."[14] Some

---

10 2 Thessalonians 2:2-3.

11 2 Thessalonians 2:9-11.

12 Acts 13:38-39; Galatians 2:16, 21; 5:1; Philippians 3:8-9.

13 Revelation 2:2.

14 Revelation 2:9.

Jews even claimed that the eagerly anticipated resurrection of the righteous had already occurred;[15] consequently, the purpose of the sacrament—remembrance of the sacrifice and atonement of Christ—was soon distorted.[16]

The event that did the most to precipitate the Great Apostasy was the death of the Apostles. The prophesied persecution of the Twelve began to take

> The demise of the Lord's Apostles led to the Great Apostasy.

its toll early, first with James, who was beheaded by Herod Agrippa I,[17] and then with the rest of the Apostles (except John) as they were pursued, captured, and killed. The need for their continued presence was best exemplified by Paul who, after fourteen years of absence preaching the gospel in other lands, returned to Jerusalem and immediately met with his fellow brethren to make sure his doctrine was still correct.[18]

A.D. 70 to A.D. 325

As the Apostles proselyted throughout the countries bordering the Mediterranean, they called local authorities to oversee the newly formed branches of the church. Since they were able to return to these local branches less and less often before their deaths, it was left to the local leaders to sustain the activity of the membership and maintain the doctrinal integrity of the gospel. By circa A.D. 101, all of the Apostles had either been killed or (in the case of John) translated by the Lord. Without central authority to govern the branches, they were left to their own resources and as a result, doctrinal divisions began to occur.

By the middle of the second century, a bishop had been established over each of the surviving church branches. By the end of the second century, the evolving church had progressed through what has been described as the "de-

---

15   2 Timothy 2:18.

16   1 Corinthians 11:19-22.

17   Acts 12:2.

18   Galatians 2:2.

velopment approach," a system of authority based on its developing creed: i.e., the evolvement of its hierarchy of bishops, priests, deacons, etc., and their interpretation of the scriptures. By this time, the branches had all rejected the necessity of apostolic authority on the argument that if they (the Apostles) were in charge, why had they disappeared? The bishops rationalized that since the original bishops had been appointed by the Lord's Apostles, the current bishops "stood in legitimate succession in a line reaching back to the Apostles themselves."[19] They therefore considered themselves to be the protectors of both the oral traditions of the branch and its developing canon of scripture.

Without central authority, doctrinal divisions continued to escalate in the fledgling church until even the position of Christ's relationship with the Father was challenged.[20] This internal, spiritual conflict became extensive, but the church was sustaining an even greater disruptive influence from without.

Rome!

At that time, Rome was the center of the world and maintained powerful legions to enforce its authority. With the exception of some early periods of relative peace, it persecuted the Christians relentlessly until the reign of Constantine. The unfortunate Christians were therefore being bombarded by the Jews because they taught Christ, and persecuted by the Roman Empire because it considered them to be a threat to its Pax Romana existence.

> The churches the Lord's Apostles established rejected the need for apostolic authority.

After Constantine became Emperor of Rome, he adopted Christianity as the state religion. One of several stories about Constantine's conversion states that he received a vision of Christ and was told in the vision to ornament

---

19 CHCC 39-44.

20 CHCC 51.

his soldiers' shields with the Savior's monogram —the Greek letters *chi* and *rho*. He obliged, and then won the battle that made him emperor of all Rome. Another version of his conversion states that both he and his entire army saw a luminous cross appear in the afternoon sky bearing the message, "In this conquer."[21] According to this account, the vision inspired Constantine to adopt Christ and to have a symbolic cross painted on the shields of his troops. In reality, however, he used both the Christian and the pagan religions to solidify his political power, and he did not personally adopt Christianity until his final illness, circa A.D. 337.[22] Nonetheless, Constantine did make Christianity the state religion of Rome and was determined to resolve the differences that had developed in Christian doctrine so as to ensure peace—both within the church and throughout the Roman empire. Unfortunately, his powerful influence and his assistance in resolving doctrinal conflicts within the church ultimately resulted in its complete apostasy from the truth—an apostasy that had been developing for more than two centuries.

> Constantine's attempt to resolve doctrinal differences in the church resulted in a complete apostasy from the truth.

Constantine's efforts to unify Christianity resulted in the calling of the Council of Nicaea.[23] Somewhere around May 20, A.D. 325, approximately 220 bishops met to resolve their doctrinal differences, regulate authority, and develop a religious creed. The council of Nicaea and the councils that followed after Constantine's death culminated in the Constantinople Council, circa A.D. 381. Prior to the meeting of these ecumenical councils, however, political factions elevated the authority of the churches of Rome, Antioch, and Alexandria over that of the other churches. The

---

21   CHCC 50.
22   CC 664; CHCC 50.
23   CC 559.

fourth Canon of the Council of Nicaea declared that these three churches were now the supreme ruling entities of the Christian church. Rome soon became the most prominent among these three because it was the capital of the empire, possessed great wealth (it had assisted many of the other churches financially), and was reputed historically as the last place Peter and Paul had taught. It was also considered the place of their martyrdom and burial.[24]

This centralization of authority in Rome eventually developed into the supreme papal authority of Western Christendom. "These powerful papal monarchs . . . controlled a vast ecclesiastical machinery that regulated in minute detail the moral and social behavior of medieval men—kings and princes as well as peasants and townspeople."[25]

After the Constantinople Council of A.D. 381, the remains of the original church vanished and the apostate church "erected a durable structure of authority, a framework of steel that has enabled it to meet every conceivable crisis."[26] Controversies over the doctrine involving God, the Son of God, and the Holy Ghost were resolved into what has become known as the Nicaean Creed. Under the Creed, the three identifiable deities revealed in the scriptures became an all-in-one entity—mysterious and unidentifiable.[27] The creed was later formalized and adopted into what became known as the Creed of Constantinople.[28]

Paul had prophesied to Timothy that the time would come when "sound doctrine" would not be endured and the truth would be turned into "fables."[29] By A.D. 381, that time had arrived. Christianity did not succeed in destroying

> Christ's original church vanished after the Constantinople Council of A.D. 381.

---

24   CHCC 46.
25   CHCC 11.
26   CHCC 45.
27   SC 250, ftnt 15.
28   SC 250, ftnt 16.
29   2 Timothy 4:3-4.

paganism—it simply adopted it![30] Thus, the falling away prophesied by Paul was complete.

Early in the fourth century as the apostasy of Christianity on the Eastern Hemisphere was progressing toward its apex, the apostasy of the tribes of Joseph (Ephraim and Manasseh) on the Western Hemisphere was not far behind. After the Savior appeared on the Western Hemisphere following His resurrection (all of the wicked there having been killed during the destruction that occurred when He was crucified),[31] the church enjoyed two hundred years of peace and righteousness. But with the deaths of those who had been personal witnesses of the Savior, the seeds of apostasy again began to grow.

However, the Saints on the Western Hemisphere did not have the fundamental problems faced by church members in the East. There were no Gentiles with pagan ways to spread their influence. Instead, sins connected with worldliness opened a chasm that eventually lead to their rejection of the gospel, their apostasy from the truth, and their total destruction of the righteous. The Book of Mormon testifies that there began to be "pride, . . . the wearing of costly apparel, . . . [and a desire for] the fine things of the world." The people "began to be divided into classes; . . . to build up churches unto themselves to get gain, and . . . to deny the true church of Christ." They "wilfully [rebelled] against the gospel of Christ" and became exceedingly wicked.[32] In another hundred years, they also would be in complete apostasy.

The Old Testament prophet Isaiah foresaw the full apostasy of all the tribes of Israel.[33] He declared that it

> Apostasy on the Western Hemisphere was not far behind apostasy on the Eastern Hemisphere.

---

30   CC 595.

31   3 Nephi 8.

32   4 Nephi 1:24, 26, 38, 45.

33   Isaiah 5:3-19.

would occur because the people would transgress the laws, change the ordinances, and break the everlasting covenant of Abraham.[34] The prophet Amos prophesied that a famine would occur to all Israel (and by adoption, to the Gentiles), "not a famine of bread, nor a thirst for water, but of hearing the words of the Lord." He further prophesied that the people of Israel would "wander from sea to sea, and from the north even to the east," that they would "run to and fro to seek the word of the Lord, and [would] not find it."[35]

As prophesied by John the Revelator, with the advent of the Great Apostasy the devil's fight for dominion over the people of the earth began anew.[36] And when the prophesied apostasy was complete, the times of the Gentiles were ushered in.

Proselyting Helps

The church Christ organized and the gospel He restored during the meridian of time fell into complete apostasy, as biblical and historical evidences verify:

Biblical
- Isaiah foresaw the full apostasy of all the tribes of Israel. The people would transgress the laws, change the ordinances, and break the everlasting covenant of Abraham.

- Amos prophesied that the Israelites would suffer a famine—not of food or of water, but of hearing the words of the Lord.

- Peter prophesied that the church Christ established in

---

34   Isaiah 24:5.

35   Amos 8:11-12.

36   Revelation 12:12-17.

the meridian of time would not survive and that a restoration of the gospel must take place before the Second Coming.

- Paul wrote that the Second Coming would not occur until after the devil had caused an apostasy from the truth.

- The disappearance of the Apostles greatly fueled the apostasy.

- The churches (or branches) were left on their own after the deaths of the Apostles, and it was left to the local leaders to sustain the activity of the membership and maintain the doctrinal integrity of the gospel. Without central authority, doctrinal divisions began to occur.

The Book of Mormon

- The apostasy of the tribes of Ephraim and Manasseh on the Western Hemisphere was not far behind that occurring on the Eastern Hemisphere.

- Christ appeared to the righteous remnant living on the Western Hemisphere after His crucifixion, but after the deaths of those who had personally witnessed the Savior, the seeds of apostasy began to grow.

- Sins connected with worldliness eventually lead the people of the Western Hemisphere to reject the gospel and go into complete apostasy.

Historical

- By the end of the second century after Christ, the "development approach," a system of authority based on a developing creed, was established in the church branches.

- All branches rejected the necessity of apostolic authority.

- Constantine became Emperor of Rome and adopted Christianity as the state religion.

- Constantine's efforts to unify Christianity ultimately resulted in the Councils of Nicaea and Constantinople. As a result of these Councils, the Godhead became an all-in-one entity and the falling away prophesied by Paul became complete.

The above summary and the biblical references from the chapter can help our friends and neighbors understand that not only did a worldwide apostasy from the truth occur, it was prophesied throughout the scriptures.

The Times of the Gentiles

The fulfillment of the times of the Gentiles is another evidence of the Restoration. These times came to an end when the Lord restored His gospel to Joseph Smith in the early 1800s.

As a result of the Great Apostasy, the light of the gospel that Jesus had restored to the earth during His ministry was extinguished. An intellectual and spiritual darkness settled upon all

The times of the Gentiles (the Dark Ages) were prophesied by both Isaiah and Micah.

earth's inhabitants as the times of the Gentiles were ushered in. These times, commonly called the Dark Ages, were prophesied by both Isaiah and his contemporary, Micah. Isaiah warned, "Woe unto them that call evil good, and good evil; that put darkness for light, and light for darkness; that put bitter for sweet, and sweet for bitter!"[1] For "darkness shall cover the earth, and gross darkness the people."[2] Micah similarly prophesied, "Therefore night

---

1   Isaiah 5:20.

2   Isaiah 60:2.

14

shall be unto you, that ye shall not have a vision; and it shall be dark unto you, that ye shall not divine; and the sun shall go down over the prophets, and the day shall be dark over them."[3]

A .D. 325 to A.D. 1820

Many prophets described what the times of the Gentiles would be like. In the Book of Mormon, the prophet Nephi recorded that on the Western Hemisphere and on all other lands, the people would be "drunken

Prophets in the Bible and the Book of Mormon described the times of the Gentiles as a time of intellectual stagnation and moral depravity.

with iniquity and all manner of abominations."[4] Isaiah described the spiritual state of the people as "drunken, but not with wine; they stagger, but not with strong drink. For the Lord hath poured out upon [them] the spirit of deep sleep, and hath closed [their] eyes."[5] Referencing the words of Isaiah, Nephi continues. "Ye have rejected the prophets; and your rulers, and the seers hath he covered because of your iniquity." In other words, because of their apostasy, the Lord had withdrawn His prophets from them.[6]

During these dark times, the Gentiles were "a scourge" to the descendants of Joseph on the Western Hemisphere[7] and Jerusalem on the Eastern Hemisphere was "trodden down."[8] However, the promises the Lord had made through His prophets indicated that these abominable conditions would not continue forever. Paul stated this fact to the Roman Gentiles who had accepted the gospel when he said, "For I would not, brethren, that ye should be ignorant of this mystery [of why Gentiles should be allowed into the covenant], lest ye should be wise in your own conceits

---

3   Micah 3:6.
4   2 Nephi 27:1.
5   Isaiah 29:9-10.
6   2 Nephi 27:5.
7   3 Nephi 20:28.
8   Luke 21:24.

[think yourselves better than Israel]; that blindness in part is happened to Israel, *until the fulness of the Gentiles be come in.*"[9] Subsequently, the Lord rejected and scattered Israel (including those Gentiles on the Eastern Hemisphere who had come into the covenant through baptism) until the time of the fullness of the Gentiles was complete.

Just as he prophesied of the vast darkness that would befall the people of the earth, Isaiah predicted the time that *light* would eventually return: "[T] he Gentiles shall come to thy light, and kings to the brightness of thy rising."[10] Thus it was that with the advent of universities and the expansion of knowledge in the eleventh century, intellectual light finally began to dispel the Dark Ages. Spiritual enlightenment increased following Martin Luther's revolt against the authority of the Holy Roman Empire in the sixteenth century and John Calvin, usually referred to as the architect of Protestantism, further energized Luther's revolt. His biblical commentaries formulated the doctrine from which the Protestant churches arose. While most non-Lutheran churches of the time were Calvinists, they eventually split into a host of separate churches and laid the groundwork for the struggle of religious freedom that made the restoration of the gospel possible.

> Martin Luther and John Calvin paved the way for the Restoration.

The Lord declared through Isaiah that He would "proceed to do a marvellous work among [the Gentiles], even a marvellous work and a wonder."[11] This marvelous work would commence with a vision and the restoration of a book that would provide a second witness to the divinity of Jesus Christ. Nephi elaborated on this when he said the

> A "marvelous work and a wonder" commenced with a vision and the restoration of the Book of Mormon.

---

9   Romans 11:25. Emphasis added.

10   Isaiah 60:3.

11   Isaiah 29:14; see also 2 Nephi 27:26.

book would contain God's revelations from "the beginning of the world to the ending thereof"—revelations that would turn the things of the Gentiles upside down.[12] The restoration of this work would consummate only after light burst forth "among them that sit in darkness." *That light is the fullness of the Lord's gospel,[13] and in the generation that it was restored, the times of the Gentiles were fulfilled.[14]*

Proselyting Helps

The times of the Gentiles, the Dark Ages prophesied by Isaiah and Micah, followed the Great Apostasy. As enlightenment slowly returned to civilization during these centuries, the Lord started preparing mankind for the restoration of the gospel.

- Both biblical and Book of Mormon prophets described what the times of the Gentiles would be like.

  - The Gentiles would be a scourge to the remaining Israelites on both hemispheres.

  - Israel would be scattered until the times of the Gentiles were fulfilled.

  - The people would be sinful, ignorant, and irreligious.

- The prophesied Book of Mormon came forth during the Restoration and the Lord's gospel was restored. Intellectual and religious truths once more enlightened mankind.

---

12   Isaiah 29; 2 Nephi 27:6–35.

13   D&C 45:28.

14   D&C 45:30.

The fight for religious freedom by such men as Martin Luther and John Calvin laid the groundwork for the restoration of the gospel. Explaining the Reformation is another way to help nonmembers accept that the Great Apostasy did occur. It can also lead into an opportunity to share the Joseph Smith story. Explain that starting with Joseph Smith's vision of God the Father and His Son Jesus Christ in 1820, intellectual and spiritual light noticeably increased as the Restoration was ushered in.

SECTION II

Prophetic Evidences

That in the dispensation of the fulness of times he might gather together in one all things in Christ, both which are in heaven, and which are on earth; even in him.

Ephesians 1:10

Forecasting the Restoration

The similarity between Christ's ancient church and the Church of Jesus Christ of Latter-day Saints is one of the strongest evidences of the Restoration. Both had the same purposes: to fulfill prophecy, to establish the Lord's true church, and to offer salvation and exaltation to all mankind.

Approximately fifteen hundred years passed from the time the early church apostatized until the time the gospel was restored. The Savior had ascended into heaven, His Apostles (with the exception of John) were all dead, and apostasy had totally destroyed His church on both the Eastern and the Western Hemispheres. However, as the apostate "times of the Gentiles" drew to a close, the fore-appointed time of the Restoration arrived.[1] It was time for the covenant of Abraham to be reestablished and the dispensation of the fullness of times, a time "made up of all the dispen-

---

1   D&C 45:24-30.

21

sations that ever [had] been given since the world began," to be ushered in.[2]

The restoration of the gospel was foreseen by the Old Testament prophet Daniel while he was a captive of King Nebuchadnezzar. The scriptures relate that Nebuchadnezzar had had a distressing dream and was troubled to know what the dream meant—*even though he could not remember what it had been about!*[3] The king called his wise men together and asked them to interpret the dream. They said they would if the king would relate the dream to them. But Nebuchadnezzar informed them that they not only had to interpret it for him, they had to recall its contents. They immediately confessed that they were unable to do this. When the wise men could not satisfy his request, Nebuchadnezzar issued a decree condemning them to death. Having been a prophet in Israel, Daniel unfortunately fell under this decree.

> Daniel the prophet foresaw the restoration of the gospel in the latter days.

When Daniel was told that his life was in jeopardy, he went to Arioch, the captain of Nebuchadnezzar's guard, to find out why the decree had been issued. Arioch told him the circumstances, and Daniel immediately went to Nebuchadnezzar and told him that given a little time, he could recall the dream for the king and tell him what it meant. The king granted his petition and Daniel returned to his house.

That night, the Lord revealed the secret of Nebuchadnezzar's dream to Daniel in a vision. The next day he went back to Arioch and said, "Destroy not the wise men of Babylon: [but] bring me in before the king, and I will shew unto [him] the interpretation" of his dream.[4] Daniel was again admitted to the presence of the king where he related the following: "Thou, O king, [saw] a great im-

---

2   HC 3:51.

3   Daniel 2:1–9.

4   Daniel 2:24.

age [of a man] . . . whose brightness was excellent, [and it] stood before thee; and the form thereof was terrible. This image's head was of fine gold, his breast and his arms of silver, his belly and his thighs of brass, [h]is legs of iron, his feet part of iron and part of clay."[5] Daniel then explained that the man-image Nebuchadnezzar had seen represented the kingdoms of the earth. The head of gold depicted Babylon, Nebuchadnezzar's great kingdom.[6] The rest of the image is commonly assumed to comprise the empires of Persia-Medes (breast and arms of silver), Greece (belly and thighs of brass), and Rome (legs of iron). Eventually, the Roman Empire would break into ten kingdoms (described as the "feet and toes" of the man-image), ten kingdoms that would be partly strong yet partly broken—a mixture of iron and "miry clay."[7] These kingdoms, and the nations that descended from them during the Dark Ages, are historically described as the Holy Roman Empire, an empire that was held together by a religious power (the "seed of men") that derived its strength from the political prowess of the old "iron" or Roman empire.[8] However, the dream revealed that the nations of iron and clay would not "cleave" one to another. Eventually, the religious yoke that bound them together would be broken and they would become individual, secular nations.

Daniel's interpretation continued. "Thou sawest . . . that a stone was cut out without hands, which smote the image upon his feet that were of iron and clay, and brake them to pieces. Then was the iron, the clay, the brass, the silver, and the gold, broken to pieces together, and became like the chaff of the summer threshingfloors; and the wind carried them away, that no place was found for them: and

---

5   Daniel 2:31-33.
6   Daniel 2:38.
7   Daniel 2:41.
8   Daniel 2:43.

the stone that smote the image became a great mountain, and filled the whole earth."[9]

Daniel said the small stone "cut out without hands" represents God's kingdom, a kingdom that will never be destroyed.[10] And when the small

> Nebuchadnezzar's dream revealed that God's kingdom will eventually fill the whole earth.

stone smites the image and breaks all of the kingdoms of the man-image apart and becomes a "great mountain" that fills "the whole earth," it is interpreted to mean that God's kingdom will eventually supersede all national boundaries; that through the restoration of the gospel, God's power will grow until it eventually fills the whole earth.[11] Thus, long before Paul prophesied that the Second Coming would not occur until after a falling away,[12] and before Peter prophesied that all things would be restored after the apostasy,[13] Daniel envisioned the Restoration and the establishment of God's work in the latter days.

In symbolic vision, John the Revelator actually saw the restoration of the gospel taking place. He

> John saw Satan overcome Christ's ancient church.

saw the devil successfully overcome the church that Christ and His Apostles had established while they were upon the earth, followed by the passage of a long period of time.[14] Then he saw "another angel fly in the midst of heaven, having the everlasting gospel to preach unto them that dwell on the earth." Ultimately, he saw the gospel taken "to every nation, and kindred, and tongue, and people."[15]

The prophets of the Western Hemisphere recorded a much clearer vision of the miraculous events associated with the Restoration. Nephi saw the establishment of

---

9   Daniel 2:34-35.

10   Daniel 2:44.

11   Daniel 2.

12   2 Thessalonians 2:1-3.

13   Acts 3:19-21.

14   Revelation 12:5-6.

15   Revelation 14:6.

America upon the Western Hemisphere and the scattering of the seed of Lehi (the Native Americans) by Gentile settlers. After that, he saw

Nephi saw the establishment of America and the scattering of the Native Americans by Gentile settlers.

the Lord "proceed to do a marvelous work among the Gentiles," even the restoration of the gospel.[16] A descendant of Nephi, also named Nephi, recorded the following words of the Savior concerning the future gathering of the tribes of Israel (a message given to the descendants of Lehi when the Lord visited them after His resurrection). "I give unto you a sign, that ye may know the time when these things shall be about to take place."[17]

The sign the Lord gave signaling the beginning of the restoration of the gospel was the coming forth of the Book of Mormon. The Lord

Translation of the Book of Mormon signaled the beginning of the Restoration.

declared that this sign would "be made known unto the Gentiles"[18] so that they and the seed of Lehi might know that the work of the Father had already commenced "unto the fulfilling of the covenant which he hath made unto the people who are of the house of Israel."[19]

Proselyting Helps

The Lord sent visions to many individuals forecasting the Restoration. He even gave a sign signaling the beginning of the Restoration. That sign was the coming forth of the Book of Mormon.

- King Nebuchadnezzar foresaw the Restoration in a

---

16 1 Nephi 22:7-8.

17 3 Nephi 21:1.

18 3 Nephi 21:2.

19 3 Nephi 21:2,7; see also verses 1-9.

dream. He did not remember the dream nor understand its meaning until the prophet Daniel recalled the
dream for him and interpreted it.

- John the Revelator saw the devil overcome and Christ's
  church and His gospel reestablished in the latter days.

- The prophet Nephi saw the establishment of America
  and the scattering of the Native Americans by Gentile
  settlers.

- John prophesied that missionaries would take the Lord's
  gospel to every nation, kindred, tongue, and people.

All elements of the gospel given throughout the various dispensations of time were prophesied to be restored
in their entirety in the last days. These examples can be
used to show your friends that like the Great Apostasy, the
Restoration was prophesied throughout the Bible. You can
then explain to them that through the Prophet Joseph Smith,
all of this has come to pass.

And it shall come to pass . . . that I will pour out my spirit upon all flesh; and your sons and your daughters shall prophesy, your old men shall dream dreams, your young men shall see visions . . .

Joel 2:28

Visions

Visions from God are recorded in many places in the Bible and the Book of Mormon, but they appear to have ceased during the Dark Ages. When Joseph Smith received a vision of the Father and the Son in 1820, it proved that the heavens were again open—another unique evidence of the Restoration.

Adam was the last man to walk and talk face to face with God the Father, and only while he was living in the Garden of Eden. After Adam and Eve sinned, they could no longer be in the presence of the Father and were punished by being evicted from the Garden. Thereafter, God communicated with mankind through visions and revelation.

Visions from God occurred periodically throughout Old Testament times. Sometimes they occurred in the form of a dream, such as the dreams Joseph of Egypt had that portrayed his supremacy over his brothers and his parents.[1]

---

1   Genesis 37.

Sometimes, in the course of bringing the Lord's plans to fruition, those who were not prophets of God were given inspired dreams, such as Pharaoh's dream of the years of plenty and famine that served as a catalyst in preserving the people of Israel.[2] Occasionally open visions occurred, like those given to Elisha, Ezekiel, and Daniel showing the first coming of Christ, the destruction of the Jews and Jerusalem, and the Second Coming of the Messiah in the latter days. Even wicked kings could receive open visions. Belshazzar, the evil son of King Nebuchadnezzar, saw some writing on a wall which when interpreted by Daniel, told Belshazzar that God had observed his kingdom and had weighed him in the balance and found him wanting. Consequently, his reign ended and his kingdom was given to the Medes and the Persians.[3]

On another occasion, the Old Testament prophet Jacob saw a ladder full of angels who were ascending and descending as they traveled from heaven to the earth and back.[4] He also saw the Lord "face to face" in vision.[5]

Moses saw a burning bush that changed his life's mission and resulted in the Children of Israel being released from bondage in Egypt.[6] He was later privileged to envision the whole earth and all its people, as had the prophet Enoch before him.[7] Isaiah and Ezekiel saw the Lord when the Lord called them as prophets.[8] Many other recorded visions testify of the Savior and the direction He wants His people to take.

> Many Old Testament prophets received visions.

In the New Testament, Zachariah saw the angel Gabriel

---

2   Genesis 41.
3   Daniel 5:25–28.
4   Genesis 28.
5   Genesis 32:30.
6   Exodus 3:2.
7   Moses 1; 7.
8   Isaiah 6, Ezekiel 1:26–28.

at the announcement of John's birth;[9] Mary saw Gabriel six months later when the Savior's birth was an-

nounced. Joseph, Mary's husband, was given a dream telling him that he need not fear taking Mary as his wife because her pregnancy was conceived "of the Holy Ghost." He was also told that the boy child's name should be "Jesus," and that He would save His people from their sins. This fulfilled the prophecy that a virgin would be with child and would bear a son who would be called Emmanuel, "which being interpreted is, God with us."[10] This open communication with heaven continued when on another occasion, an angel appeared to Joseph in a dream and instructed him to take Mary and Jesus to Egypt because King Herod would "seek the young child to destroy him."[11]

Later, during His ministry, Jesus took Peter, James, and John up on a high mountain where they saw the Lord transfigured before them: "and his face did shine as the sun, and his raiment was white as the light."[12] They were even privileged to hear the Father bear testimony of Christ when He said, "This is my beloved Son, in whom I am well pleased; hear ye him."[13]

While being stoned to death for regaling the Jewish leaders with the fact that they were the betrayers and crucifiers of Christ, Steven—being full of the Holy Ghost— "looked up stedfastly into heaven, and saw the glory of God, and Jesus standing on the right hand of God." Those who witnessed and participated in Steven's death ironically laid their cloaks at the feet of a young man named Saul for safekeeping[14]—the same Saul whose life would be changed forever by a vision of the Lord that befell him as he trav-

---

9 Luke 1:5-20.

10 Luke 1:26-35; Isaiah 7:14.

11 Matthew 1:18-25; 2:13.

12 Matthew 17:1-8.

13 Matthew 17:5.

14 Acts 7:55-58.

eled on the road to Damascus.[15] Later, Saul (whose name was changed to Paul by the Lord) related a vision he had had of the heavens when he wrote that he "knew a man in Christ above fourteen years ago, (whether in the body, I cannot tell; or whether out of the body, I cannot tell: God knoweth;) such an one caught up to the third heaven. And I knew such a man . . . that . . . was caught up into paradise, and heard unspeakable words, which it is not lawful for a man to utter."[16]

Other great visions were given to John the Revelator and are recorded in the book of Revelation. His vi-

| John's vision encompassed the entire history of the earth.

sions cover the history of the earth, from the pre-existence to the final judgment, and reveal cataclysmic events that will occur prior to the Lord's Second Coming: two witnesses in Jerusalem whose deaths will usher in the Savior's advent; the devil's rule and the signs of his evil leaders, including the mark of the beast; the restoration and harvest of the righteous; the destruction of the devil's kingdom and his punishment; the last great cleansing of the earth; and the battle of Gog and Magog.

In the Book of Mormon, Lehi dreamed of the Tree of Life.[17] His son Nephi was privileged to not only envision his father's dream, but to interpret it (adding further insight to the vision from the information revealed to him). He saw the Redeemer and he saw John the Baptist—the prophet who prepared the way of the Lord and baptized Him.[18] Nephi's brother Jacob also saw the Lord,[19] and the Brother of Jared, Mahonri Moriancumer, saw a vision of the Lord's spirit.[20]

One of the great prophets of the Book of Mormon that

---

15   Acts 9:3-7.
16   2 Corinthians 12:2-4.
17   1 Nephi 8.
18   1 Nephi 11.
19   2 Nephi 11:3.
20   Ether 3:13-16.

30

we know little about was third Nephi, whose ministry was contemporary with Christ's. He had angels visit him daily, and was privileged to see the

Third Nephi witnessed the Savior's earthly ministry in vision.

Savior's daily ministrations. This Nephi became a surrogate Christ to the people on the Western Hemisphere and mirrored the Lord's teachings and miracles to those he taught.[21]

In spite of all this evidence proving that visions and revelations occurred (even discounting the visions contained in the Book of Mormon and the Pearl of Great Price), the churches functioning during the apostasy decided that visions had ceased. And although inspiration

Visions ceased during the Dark Ages.

from the Lord initiated the end of the Dark Ages, perhaps visions *did* in fact cease during that long period of spiritual sleep.

This all changed in A.D. 1820. In answer to his sincere prayer to know which church he should join, fourteen-year-old Joseph Smith received a startling, glorious vision of God the Father and His Son, Jesus Christ.

The Joseph Smith Story

Young Joseph was living with his family in Palmyra, New York, at a time when there was a great deal of religious excitement in the area. He had listened to various claims from the revivalists in and around Palmyra, but was confused as to which church was true. His mother and several of his brothers and sisters had decided to associate with the Presbyterian faith, while he became partial to the Methodist sect. However, as the religious maelstrom swirled around him, he became unsure: which was right, or were they all wrong together? It was this agony of indecision that led him to delve into the Bible for answers. He came across James 1:5 which states, "If any of you lack wisdom, let him

---

21   3 Nephi 7:15-18.

ask of God, that giveth to all men liberally, and upbraideth not; and it shall be given him." This powerful passage of scripture led to Joseph's famous prayer in the Sacred Grove and the remarkable vision he received. He relates the experience in his own words:

> I retired to the woods . . . on the morning of a beautiful, clear day, early in the spring of eighteen hundred and twenty. It was the first time in my life that I had made such an attempt, for amidst all my anxieties I had never as yet made the attempt to pray vocally.
>
> After I had retired to the place where I had previously designed to go, having looked around me, and finding myself alone, I kneeled down and began to offer up the desires of my heart to God. I had scarcely done so, when immediately I was seized upon by some power which entirely overcame me, and had such an astonishing influence over me as to bind my tongue so that I could not speak. Thick darkness gathered around me, and it seemed to me for a time as if I were doomed to sudden destruction.
>
> But, exerting all my powers to call upon God to deliver me out of the power of this enemy which had seized upon me, and at the very moment when I was ready to sink into despair and abandon myself to destruction—not to an imaginary ruin, but to the power of some actual being from the unseen world, who had such marvelous power as I had never before felt in any being—just at this moment of great alarm, I saw a pillar of light exactly over my head, above the bright-

ness of the sun, which descended gradually until it fell upon me.

It no sooner appeared than I found myself delivered from the enemy which held me bound. When the light rested upon me I saw two Personages, whose brightness and glory defy all description, standing above me in the air. One of them spake unto me, calling me by name and said, pointing to the other—*This is My Beloved Son. Hear Him!*[22]

> Joseph Smith had a vision of God the Father and His Son, Jesus Christ.

The Lord then told Joseph that all of the churches upon the earth at that time were wrong; he must not join any of them. Their creeds were an abomination in His sight and their leaders corrupt, only drawing near to God with their lips while their hearts were far from Him. The Lord informed Joseph that these professors of religion were teaching for doctrine the commandments of men, "having a form of godliness, but [denying] the power thereof."[23] Joseph heeded the Lord's council, joined none of the churches, and waited patiently for further instructions.

In his innocence, Joseph related the circumstances of his vision to one of the Methodist preachers with whom he was acquainted, and was astounded at the man's reaction. The religionist told him with great contempt that the vision was of the devil, "that there were no such things as visions or revelations . . . that all such things had ceased with the Apostles, and that there would never be any more of them."[24]

From this point on, Joseph suffered persecution from doubters, antagonists, and enemies, but he never denied

---

22 Joseph Smith - History 1:14-17.

23 Joseph Smith - History 1:19.

24 Joseph Smith - History 1: 21.

having seen a vision and he never denied receiving revelations from God. Sadly, the atmosphere of hate and distrust generated by his testimony eventually led to his martyrdom, but his untimely death did not put an end to the criticism, opposition, and disbelief of his testimony or the church he established—even to the present day.

Joseph's vision produced amazing results: it revoked the Nicene Creed, closed the Dark Ages, initiated the end of the times of the Gentiles, proved the veracity of the Bible, and began the restoration of all things. Is it any wonder that the devil attempted to destroy him and prevent the restoration of the gospel after the Lord had told him in vision not to join any of the existing religions of his day?[25]

Proselyting Helps

Visions occurred anciently, as the Bible and the Book of Mormon testify. They can come in various forms:

- Pharaoh's vision of the years of plenty and the years of famine that would befall Egypt came in the form of an inspired dream.

- A burning bush changed Moses' life when the Lord called him to free the Israelites from slavery in Egypt. He later received an open vision of the entire world and all its people.

- Zachariah and Mary saw the angel Gabriel in vision.

- Peter, James, and John witnessed the Savior's transfiguration.

- Through the power of the Holy Ghost, Steven saw the glory of God and Jesus standing on His right hand.

25   HC 1:1-8.

- Paul had a vision of the heavens.

- John the Revelator's vision covered the entire history of the earth, from the pre-existence to the final judgment.

- Third Nephi in the Book of Mormon was a contemporary of Jesus Christ and witnessed the Savior's daily ministrations.

- A vision of the Father and the Son was given to Joseph Smith to usher in the Restoration.

Church functionaries during the apostasy decided visions had ceased. The fact that the Lord is again giving visions to his latter-day prophets is another unique evidence of the Restoration.

The Book of Mormon

The Lord gave a sign indicating that the Restoration of all things had commenced. The
sign he gave was the coming forth of the Book
of Mormon, a voice from the dust.

When speaking of the gathering of Israel in double-ref-
erence prophecy, the Old Testament prophet Ezekiel described two written records that would come forth: one
from the tribe of Judah (the Bible), and the other from the
tribe of Joseph (the Book of Mormon). He called these records "sticks," and the Lord commanded him to take one
stick and write upon it for "Judah, and for the children of
Israel his companions," and to take the second stick and
write upon it for "Joseph, the stick of Ephraim, and for all
the house of Israel his companions." He then commanded
Ezekiel to "join them one to another into one stick," noting
that they would become "one in thine hand."[1] Both sticks

---

1   Ezekiel 37:16–17.

36

are united in purpose; both records testify of our Lord and Savior Jesus Christ.

Isaiah also prophesied of the Book of Mormon when he indicated that the voices of Book of Mormon prophets would "speak out of the ground," and would "whisper out of the dust."[2] This prophesy was very literally fulfilled when Joseph Smith retrieved the gold plates from the hill Cumorah, buried there centuries earlier by the prophet Moroni.

Isaiah gave a second, very specific prophecy regarding the coming forth of the Book of Mormon. While referring to the Great Apostasy, he wrote,

> Stay yourselves, and wonder; cry yet out, and cry: they are drunken, but not with wine; they stagger, but not with strong drink.
>
> For the Lord hath poured out upon you the spirit of deep sleep, and hath closed your eyes: the prophets and your rulers, the seers hath he covered.
>
> And the vision of all is become unto you as the words of a book that is sealed, which men deliver to one that is learned, saying, Read this, I pray thee: and he saith, I cannot; for it is sealed:
>
> And the book is delivered to him that is not learned, saying, Read this, I pray thee: and he saith, I am not learned.[3]

We recognize today that in addition to the general Restoration, Isaiah was seeing very specific incidents that occurred during the translation of the Book of Mormon: Martin Harris asking Professor Charles Anthon to authen-

2   Isaiah 29:4.
3   Isaiah 29:9–12.

ticate the hieroglyphics from the gold plates, and Joseph initially feeling inadequate at the task of translation because he was uneducated.

Isaiah's prophecy continued:

> Therefore, behold, I will proceed to do a marvellous work among this people, even a marvellous work and a wonder: for the wisdom of their wise men shall perish, and the understanding of their prudent men shall be hid. . . .
>
> And in that day shall the deaf hear the words of the book, and the eyes of the blind shall see out of obscurity, and out of darkness.[4]

The marvelous work the Lord refers to in Isaiah was not only the restoration of the gospel, but the coming forth of the Book of Mormon and the enlightenment the world would receive when the message of its pages was promulgated.

The Lord himself in His good shepherd sermon declared to the Jews that He had *other sheep* than the tribe of Judah that | The Lord visited tribes other than Judah.

He must visit. "[T]hem also I must bring," He declared, "and they shall hear my voice; and there shall be one fold, and one shepherd."[5] The sheep He was referring to were the other tribes of Israel, among them the tribe of Joseph (a remnant of which was living on the Western Hemisphere at the time). After the Lord's resurrection, He visited the Western Hemisphere and confirmed to the Nephite people that they were the ones He had been referring to.[6] This appears to confirm the blessing Father Israel gave his cherished son

---

4   Isaiah 29: 14, 18.

5   John 10:16.

6   3 Nephi 15:21-24.

Joseph prior to Israel's death. He prophesied that Joseph's descendants would be "a fruitful bough, even a fruitful bough by a well; whose branches run over the wall," indicating that Joseph's descendants would eventually stretch beyond the confines of the promised land of Canaan and the oceanic boundaries that surrounded the Eastern Hemisphere, and dwell on the Western Hemisphere.[7]

Finally, John the Revelator had a vision wherein he saw "another angel fly in the midst of heaven, having the everlasting gospel to preach unto them that dwell on the earth, and to every nation, and kindred, and tongue, and people."[8] This passage has always been interpreted by the Church to refer to the angel Moroni, and by extension, to his interaction with the Prophet Joseph Smith.

Origin of the Book of Mormon: A.D. 1823–1829

As a result of prayerful inquiry concerning which church he should join, 14-year-old Joseph Smith received a vision in 1820 in which he saw God the Father and His son, Jesus Christ. They informed him that none of the churches of his time were correct and that he must not join any of them. Satisfied for the moment, Joseph did not affiliate with any church and continued to pursue the common vocations of life. Once he told others of his vision, however, he began to suffer "severe persecution at the hands of all classes of men, both religious and irreligious," a circumstance that caused him great consternation.[9]

Three years later, on the evening of September 21, 1823, Joseph prayed and asked God to forgive him for all his sins and follies and to give him some type of a manifestation so that he would know his standing before Him. The result was the first of several visits by the angel Moroni, the same

---

7   Genesis 49:22.

8   Revelation 14:6.

9   Joseph Smith – History 1:28.

angel John the Revelator had seen in vision.[10] The angel quoted several verses from Chapters 3 and 4 of Malachi[11] and told Joseph that God had work for him to do. He revealed that Joseph's name would be held for both good and evil among all nations, kindreds, and tongues; in other words, he would be spoken of both for good and for evil among all civilizations (not unlike Paul when the Lord had Ananias heal him and then showed him the great things he would suffer for the Lord's sake).[12]

After this disconcerting introduction, Moroni told Joseph that a book written on gold plates was hidden in a hill near his home. He said the book contained an "account of the former inhabitants of this continent and the sources from whence they sprang." It also contained the "fullness of the everlasting Gospel" which the Savior had taught to those ancient inhabitants, and a device called the Urim and Thummim—two stones in silver bows, fastened to a breastplate. Those who had possessed the Urim and Thummim anciently were known as "Seers," and the device was now to be used in the translation of the gold plates because the "fullness of the Gentiles was soon to come in."[13] Joseph was told that he would not receive the plates immediately, but that when he did have them in his possession, he was not to show them to anyone unless he was commanded to do so. Finally, Moroni showed Joseph in a vision exactly where the plates were located.

> Moroni revealed the location of gold plates containing the history of an ancient people.

Moroni appeared to Joseph three more times, giving him essentially the same message. He warned him that "Satan would try to tempt" him because of the indigent circumstances of his family, and stressed that Joseph's only

10   Joseph Smith - History 1:30.

11   The quotes from Malachi 4:1, 5-6 vary a little from the way they read in the King James Bible. See HC 1:12 for details.

12   Acts 9:16.

13   HC 1:12-13.

objective in receiving the plates was to build the kingdom of God.

After Joseph related these experiences to his father, his father told him to do whatever the angel instructed.[14] So following Moroni's directions, Joseph immediately hiked to the spot where he knew the plates were hidden. He described the experience as follows:

> Convenient to the village of Manchester, Ontario county, New York, stands a hill of considerable size, and the most elevated of any in the neighborhood. On the west side of this hill, not far from the top, under a stone of considerable size, lay the plates, deposited in a stone box. This stone was thick and rounding in the middle on the upper side, and thinner towards the edges, so that the middle part of it was visible above the ground, but the edge all around was covered with earth.
>
> Having removed the earth, I obtained a lever, which I got fixed under the edge of the stone, and with a little exertion raised it up. I looked in, and there indeed did I behold the plates, the Urim and Thummim, and the breastplate, as stated by the messenger. The box in which they lay was formed by laying stones together in some kind of cement. In the bottom of the box were laid two stones crosswise of the box, and on these stones lay the plates and the other things with them.[15]

It would be another four years before Moroni would

14 HC 1:11-15.
15 HC 1:15-16.

allow Joseph to remove the plates. During this time, he met and courted Emma Hale and on January 18, 1827, they eloped. Thereafter, they returned to the Smith family farm where on September 22, 1827, the angel Moroni finally gave Joseph possession of the gold plates. It was not long before word went abroad that Joseph had the plates and as persecution increased, "every stratagem that could be invented was resorted to" to steal the plates from him.[16] However, Joseph successfully kept the plates safe and when he had finished translating them, he returned them to the angel Moroni.

Prophecies Fulfilled

Three prophecies were fulfilled during the translation of the gold plates:

> *And the vision of all is become unto you as the words of a book that is sealed, which men deliver to one that is learned, saying, Read this, I pray thee: and he saith, I cannot; for it is sealed:*
>
> Isaiah 29:11

Joseph sent Martin Harris to New York City with a copy of some of the characters from the plates with the intent of authenticating them. Martin first went to Dr. Samuel L.

> Martin Harris fulfilled Isaiah's prophecy when he sought to authenticate characters from the gold plates.

Mitchell, who gave him a letter of introduction to Professor Charles Anthon requesting that he review the characters and "decipher [them], if possible."[17] Martin reported that Professor Anthon authenticated the characters and gave him a certificate stating the same. The professor then asked Martin where the characters came from. Martin told him of the angelic visit by Moroni and indicated that a portion of the record was sealed and had not been translated. Pro-

---

16   HC 1:18.

17   HC 1:20 ftnt.

fessor Anthon then retrieved the certificate he had given Martin and tore it up, saying he could not read a "sealed book"—which fulfilled the prophecy in Isaiah 29:11. Martin then returned to Dr. Mitchell, who proceeded to verbally authenticate the characters.[18]

* * *

> . . . [A]fter I had made an abridgement from the plates of Nephi, down to the reign of this king Benjamin . . . I found these plates, which contained this small account of the prophets, from Jacob down to the reign of this king Benjamin . . . I chose these things to finish my record . . . I do this for a wise purpose; for thus it whispereth me, according to the workings of the Spirit of the Lord which is in me. And now, I do not know all things; but the Lord knoweth all things which are to come; wherefore, he worketh in me to do according to his will.
>
> Words of Mormon 3–7

In compiling the record on the golden plates, the prophet Mormon describes records that contained a small account of the prophets, from Jacob down to the reign of King Benjamin, as well as some of the writings of Nephi. Mormon felt these were choice records, and he chose to include them despite some duplication with what he had already compiled. As the following account verifies, the Lord was obviously aware of the fact that a portion of Joseph Smith's translation of the Book of Mormon would eventually become lost.

After translating the first 116 pages of the Book of Mormon manuscript, Martin Harris, who was acting as scribe | **Martin Harris lost 116 pages of translation.** | during most of this process, requested that he be allowed to show the record to his family. Joseph inquired of the Lord and was told no. A second inquiry was made at Martin's request, and again the Lord refused to let him take the pages. Martin implored Joseph to ask a third time, which

---

18 HC 1:20.

he did. The Lord finally granted Martin's request on the condition that he only show the pages to his wife, his father and mother, his brother (Preserved Harris), and Mrs. Cobb, the sister of Martin's wife. Martin took the record, but eventually lost it. The result was that the Urim and Thummim and the plates were taken from Joseph. When the angel finally returned the Urim and Thummim, Joseph inquired of his standing before the Lord. As a result, he received Section 3 of the Doctrine and Covenants wherein the Lord told him that God's work could not be frustrated. The Lord chastised Joseph and told him to fear God more than man. Had he trusted the Lord, the Lord would have supported him "against all the fiery darts of the adversary." The Prophet was told that God had chosen him to do His work, but if he did that which was contrary to the commandments he had been given, he would become as other men and lose the gift of translation. It was his disobedience that had caused him to lose his privileges for a season. Nevertheless, Section 3 made it clear that the Lord's work would continue to go forth:

> ... [I]nasmuch as the knowledge of a Savior has come unto the world, through the testimony of the Jews, even so shall the knowledge of a Savior come unto my people—
> And to the Nephites, and the Jacobites, and the Josephites, and the Zoramites, through the testimony of their fathers . . . and to the knowledge of the Lamanites, and the Lemuelites, and the Ishmaelites, who dwindled in unbelief because of the iniquity of their fathers . . . that the Lamanites might come to the knowledge of their fathers, and that they might know the promises of the

Lord . . . and that through their repentance
they might be saved.[19]

At the conclusion of the revelation, the angel again took
the plates and the Urim and Thummim. He gave Joseph
a few days to reconsider his position before he returned
them. Joseph again asked what the Lord wanted him to
do and in response, he received the revelation contained
in Section 10 of the Doctrine and Covenants directing him
to translate from the small plates of Nephi rather than re-
translate what he had written on the 116 pages. The Lord
knew that conspiring men had modified Joseph's original
translation and were lying in wait to accuse him of being
unable to translate the same thing over again. As a result
of this experience, the first edition of the Book of Mormon
contained a "Preface," a disclaimer explaining what had
happened as a result of the 116 pages of translation being
lost.[20]

* * *

*. . . In the mouth of two or three witnesses shall every word
be established.*

2 Corinthians 13:1

---

19 D&C 3:16-20.

20 The "Preface" in its entirety can be read at HC 1:56-57. Loss of the 116
pages of manuscript was not the adversary's only attempt to discredit the
Book of Mormon. During the printing of the book, one Esquire Cole, the ex-
justice of the peace in the Palmyra area, attempted to nefariously use each
day's printing of Joseph's translation. Cole had an arrangement with the
printer that allowed him to use the press at night to print his weekly news-
letter, the *Dogberry Paper*. This gave him access to the Book of Mormon
pages that were being printed each day. It was his intent to mutilate the
writing and publish it in his paper in order to discredit both the book and Joseph Smith. Somehow, Hyrum and Oliver discovered what he was doing and
although Joseph was in Pennsylvania at the time, they had him immediately
return and threaten suit as the copyright holder. Thus, the plot was foiled
and the integrity of the Book of Mormon was preserved. Later, the citizens
of Palmyra passed a resolution agreeing not to purchase the book after its
publication, and to use their influence to prevent others from purchasing it
as well. This caused the publisher, E.B. Grandin, to stop printing the manuscript for fear he would never be paid. Once again, Joseph had to return
from Pennsylvania and along with Martin Harris, convinced Grandin that the
printing would be paid for (HC 1:75 ftnt, 76 ftnt). As a result, Grandin finished printing the initial five thousand copies of the Book of Mormon at a
cost of $3,000.

During the process of translation, it was discovered that three witnesses should be called to testify of both the gold plates and the record they contained. Moroni recorded this requirement in "The Book of Ether":

> And behold, ye may be privileged that ye may show the plates unto those who shall assist to bring forth this work;
>
> And unto three shall they be shown by the power of God; wherefore they shall know of a surety that these things are true.
>
> And in the mouth of three witnesses shall these things be established; and the testimony of three, and this work, in the which shall be shown forth the power of God and also his word, of which the Father, and the Son, and the Holy Ghost bear record—and all this shall stand as a testimony against the world at the last day.[21]

This was not a new requirement. It is clearly stated in both the Old and New Testaments that in the mouth of "two or three witnesses shall every word be established."[22] To fulfill this requirement, Martin Harris, Oliver Cowdery, and David Whitmer requested the privilege of being the three witnesses to the Book of Mormon. After being selected, they accompanied Joseph Smith into a nearby wood where they knelt in prayer. Initially nothing happened, so Martin Harris, assuming he was the cause of the problem due to his previous loss of the 116 pages of transcript, withdrew himself from the group. A vision then opened to Joseph, Oliver, and David, and they were privileged to witness the angel Moroni and the golden plates. Joseph then sought out Martin who was praying a short distance away. He

---

21   Ether 5:2-4, see also 2 Nephi 11:3.

22   2 Corinthians 13:1; Deuteronomy 17:6; Deuteronomy 19:15; Matthew 18:16.

also was privileged to receive the vision and declared, "Tis enough; 'tis enough; mine eyes have beheld; mine eyes have beheld." Then jumping up he shouted, "Hosanna."[23]

Although these men viewed both the angel and the plates, they were not allowed to handle the plates. Moroni turned each page, however, so that they could observe them. Then a voice from heaven stated, "These plates have been revealed by the power of God, and they have been translated by the power of God. The translation of them which you have seen is correct, and I command you to bear record of what you now see and hear." This they did, and the testimony of these three witnesses continues to be printed in each copy of the Book of Mormon to this day.

In addition to these three witnesses, eight additional witnesses—Christian Whitmer; Jacob Whitmer; Peter Whitmer, Jun.; John Whitmer; Hiram Page; Joseph Smith, Sen.; Hyrum Smith; and Samuel H. Smith—also bore testimony to the Book of Mormon. The Prophet gives no detailed information pertaining to the viewing of the plates by the eight witnesses, merely noting in his records that the testimony was given. However his mother, Lucy Mack Smith, notes that the eight gathered at the Smith home and then retired to the woods where Joseph showed the brethren the plates and allowed them to handle them. In contrast to the three witnesses, there were no angelic ministrations and no heavenly confirmations of the correctness of the translation.[24]

Eleven witnesses fulfilled Paul's prophecy.

In compliance with the Lord's requirements, the testimonies of both the three and the eight witnesses were placed on the last two pages of the first edition of the Book of Mormon. In subsequent editions, they have been placed

---

23 HC 1:52-55.

24 HC 1:57 ftnt, 58 ftnt.

at the front of the book, right after the title page, where they are highly visible.

Old Testament, New Testament, and Book of Mormon prophets all testified of the coming forth of the Book of Mormon and of incidents that would occur during its translation. As this chapter shows, all of these prophecies were fulfilled—concrete evidence of the truthfulness of the Lord's great latter-day Restoration.

PROSELYTING HELPS

The Old Testament prophet Ezekiel described two records that would be available to mankind in the latter days: the Bible from the tribe of Judah, and the Book of Mormon from the tribe of Joseph. He called these records "sticks" and was directed by the Lord to join them "one to another" because of their united purpose. Both records testify of Jesus Christ, our Lord and Savior.

- The Lord made it clear that He had "other sheep" besides the tribe of Judah that He must visit. Among others, He was referring to the descendants of Lehi, a Book of Mormon prophet. The Book of Mormon recounts the history of these and other ancient Israelites who lived on the Western Hemisphere.

- Joseph Smith was instrumental in bringing forth the "stick of Joseph" in the early 1800s. Many prophecies were fulfilled when he received a vision of the angel Moroni, retrieved and translated the gold plates, and published the Book of Mormon.

- The Lord knew Joseph would face tribulations translating the gold plates, such as when Martin Harris lost 116 pages of the translated manuscript.

- Three witnesses (Martin Harris, Oliver Cowdery, and David Whitmer) were called to testify of the gold plates and the record they contained.
- Eight additional witnesses bore testimony to the truthfulness of the Book of Mormon.

The Book of Mormon, and the fact that it was translated by Joseph Smith from gold plates revealed to him by an angel, have caused some to question the LDS faith. But the fact remains that the book was prophesied to come forth in the Restoration. Even the angel who led Joseph to the plates was seen in vision by John the Revelator. However, those who read the book and earnestly pray to know if it is authentic will be able to resolve this dilemma. The Spirit will bear witness to them that the Book of Mormon is true. We can help them by explaining the prophecies and encouraging them to follow the promise found in Moroni 10:4 to receive their own witness.

The Priesthood and Baptism

No church can claim to be true if it does not have the authority to act in God's name. This authority was restored to the Church of Jesus Christ of Latter-day Saints during the Restoration.

Authority has always been necessary for mankind to act in God's name. Unauthorized individuals who attempt to act in God's name often suffer severe consequences. When King Saul improperly offered a sacrifice before going to war with the Philistines, the prophet Samuel angrily confronted him.

"What hast thou done?" he exclaimed.

"Because I saw that the people were scattered from me, and that thou camest not within the days appointed, and that the Philistines gathered themselves together at Michmash . . . [and would] come down now upon me to Gilgal, and I [had] not made supplication unto the Lord: I forced myself therefore, and offered a burnt offering," Saul explained.

"Thou hast done foolishly," Samuel replied. "Thou hast not kept the commandment of the Lord thy God . . .

for . . . the Lord [would] have established thy kingdom upon Israel for ever. But now thy kingdom shall not continue. . . ."[1]

On another occasion, Simon the sorcerer observed Peter bestowing the | Priesthood authority cannot be usurped. | Holy Ghost on repentant individuals by the laying on of hands. He offered Peter money to obtain that authority. But Peter rebuked him saying, "Thy money perish with thee, because thou hast thought that the gift of God may be purchased with money. Thou hast neither part nor lot in this matter: for thy heart is not right in the sight of God. Repent therefore of this thy wickedness, and pray God, if perhaps the thought of thine heart may be forgiven thee."[2]

A third example of the misuse of authority involves Paul the Apostle after his arrival in Ephesus. He found approximately twelve disciples there who had been baptized, and asked them if they had received the Holy Ghost. Their response was surprising.

"We have not so much as heard whether there be any Holy Ghost."

Paul immediately recognized that whoever had baptized them was not of the church and did not have the authority to baptize, so he asked them, "Unto what then were ye baptized?"

"Unto John's baptism," they replied.

Paul knew this was incorrect. He recognized that whoever had baptized them had falsely claimed to have John's authority, so he explained

"John [having authority] verily baptized with the baptism of repentance, saying unto the people that they should believe on him which should come after him, that is, on Christ Jesus."

Paul then proceeded to rebaptize the disciples and "laid his hands upon them" in confirmation, and the Holy

---

1   1 Samuel 13:9-14.

2   Acts 8:13-22.

Ghost fell upon them and they "spake in tongues, and prophesied."[3]

Paul continued proselyting in Asia for about two years, performing many great miracles. He even sent handkerchiefs or aprons from "his body" to be used in the healing of the sick and to cast out devils. On one occasion, certain "vagabond Jews, exorcists," the seven sons of a man named Sceva (one of the chief priests of the Jews in the area) decided to duplicate the miracles Paul was performing by attempting to exorcize evil spirits from some individuals who were possessed. Although they held no authority to perform such acts, they called upon the name of the Lord saying, "We abjure you by Jesus whom Paul preacheth," come out of the people.

But the evil spirit replied, "Jesus I know, and Paul I know; but who are ye?"

The evil spirit then "leaped on them, and overcame them, and prevailed against them," and they fled, "naked and wounded."[4]

Further evidence from the New Testament proving that proper authority is required to perform various functions of the gospel is recorded in connection with the call of the Lord's Apostles. In His last discourse to them prior to His betrayal, trial, and crucifixion, He stated, "Ye have not chosen me, but I have chosen you, and ordained you."[5] Again, when He sent the Twelve on their first mission, He gave them power to act in His name and perform the various miracles that He had been performing, including the ability to cast out unclean spirits.[6]

Finally, we again turn to Paul. In Hebrews he is teaching the Jews and recounting their history as the chosen people. When speaking of their authority to officiate under

---

3   Acts 19:1-7.

4   Acts 19:13-17.

5   John 15:16.

6   Matthew 10:1.

the law he said, "no man taketh this honour unto himself, but he that is called of God, as was Aaron."[7] He thus confirms that individuals cannot arbitrarily choose to exercise authority. They must be called by God through revelation and have that authority bestowed upon them.

Why Baptize?

Baptism is a requirement for entrance into the kingdom of God, and has been from the beginning. The scriptures show that Adam was baptized[8] and that Jesus was baptized

| Authoritative Baptism is the first requirement for entrance into the kingdom of God. |

by John the Baptist when He commenced His ministry[9]—in spite of the fact that there was a high priest officiating in Judah, and any rabbi or priest could have performed the ordinance. But the Lord went to John because He knew John had been ordained and received the proper authority to baptize.[10]

John preached the necessity of repentance before baptism if individuals were to receive forgiveness

| John the Baptist had the authority to baptize. |

for their sins, but he recognized that the Lord was sinless and needed neither repentance nor forgiveness. In fact, he felt *he* needed to be baptized by the Savior. The scriptures make it clear, however, that the Son of God did need the ordinance of baptism; even the sinless Messiah could not gain entrance into His Father's kingdom without it. He had to be baptized by someone holding the proper authority in order to "fulfil all righteousness."[11]

---

7   Hebrews 5:4.

8   Moses 6:64-65; see also 1 Corinthians 10:1-4.

9   Matthew 3:13-17.

10   John the Baptist was "baptized while he was yet in his childhood, and was ordained by the angel of God at the time he was eight days old unto this power, to overthrow the kingdom of the Jews, and to make straight the way of the Lord before the face of his people, to prepare them for the coming of the Lord, in whose hand is given all power" (D&C 84:28; Luke 1:49-80).

11   Matthew 3:14-15.

Consequently, John acceded to the Lord's baptism. And when Jesus had been baptized, He "went up straightway out of the water" (implying that He had been submersed under the water), and the Spirit descended upon Him "like a dove." Then the Father's voice testified of Christ's divinity saying, "This is my beloved Son, in whom I am well pleased."[12]

Nephi of old witnessed the baptism of the Savior in vision.[13] While using this vision to emphasize the necessity of baptism for all men and women, he was questioned about the need for the perfect Son of God to be baptized. He taught his people five basic reasons for the Savior to be baptized, and they are applicable to us all:

> There are five basic reasons why Jesus had to be baptized.

1. To show His humility before the Father.

2. To show that He is obedient to the Father and will keep His commandments.

3. To show that baptism is necessary prior to receiving the Holy Ghost.

4. To show mankind the path they need to follow to enter the Father's kingdom.

5. To invite all mankind to follow His example.

Nephi continued his instructions by exclaiming, "O then, how much more need have we, being unholy, to be baptized, yea, even by water!"[14]

And finally, Christ himself declared in John 3:5 that "Except a man be born of water and of the Spirit, he cannot enter into the kingdom of God."

---

12   Matthew 3:13-17.

13   1 Nephi 11:27.

14   2 Nephi 31:5-12.

When John the Baptist took the Savior into the waters of Jordan, he closed the door on Israel's apostate past and initiated its future. Later, when John appeared to Joseph Smith during the Restoration, he closed the door on the Dark Ages of the Great Apostasy and initiated the latter-day work of the Lord's plan of salvation.

Priesthood Authority Restored

Just as having the proper authority to act in God's name was necessary throughout biblical history, so also is it necessary in the Lord's restored latter-day Church. Baptism serves as an example of this need. While Oliver Cowdery was acting as Joseph's scribe during the translation of the Book of Mormon, they came upon text that referred to baptism for the remission of sins. Their curiosity piqued, on May 15, 1829, they retired to a nearby wood on the banks of the Susquehanna River and prayed. The result of their prayer was the appearance of an angel from God. The angel announced himself as John, the same that was called John the Baptist in the New Testament. He declared that he was acting under the direction of Peter, James, and John, the three ancient Apostles of the Lord. He then proceeded to lay his hands on the heads of both Joseph and Oliver and ordained them saying:

> The proper authority to act in God's name is as necessary today as it was anciently.

> Upon you my fellow servants, in the name of Messiah I confer the Priesthood of Aaron, which holds the keys of the ministering of angels, and of the gospel of repentance, and of baptism by immersion for the remission of sins; and this shall never be taken again from the earth, until the sons of Levi do offer again an offering unto the Lord in righteousness.[15]

---

15   D&C 13; HC 1:39.

The ordination of Joseph and Oliver to the Aaronic Priesthood initiated the reestablishment of God's priesthood authority upon the earth in the latter days. This priesthood gave them the authority to baptize, but John informed them that the Aaronic Priesthood did not give them the power to bestow the gift of the Holy Ghost. He said that authority would be given to them at a later time. He then instructed Joseph to baptize Oliver, and Oliver to baptize Joseph. After completing the baptisms, Joseph ordained Oliver to the Aaronic Priesthood and Oliver ordained Joseph, as Moroni had commanded.[16]

> John the Baptist conferred the Aaronic Priesthood on Joseph Smith and Oliver Cowdery on May 15, 1829.

As word of their activities spread, Joseph and Oliver began to preach to those who had been friendly toward them and shortly thereafter, they baptized Joseph's two brothers, Samuel and Hyrum. They also baptized David Whitmer and Peter Whitmer, Jr.[17] Thus, the ordinance of baptism, established by God from the time of Adam, was again being practiced upon the earth by those who held the proper priesthood authority.

There is no record of the exact date the promised Melchizedek Priesthood was restored, but that it was is not in question. In a letter to the Saints dated September 6, 1842, (Section 128 of the Doctrine and Covenants) Joseph stated the following:

---

16   Joseph records that after he and Oliver came out of the waters of baptism, they exercised the gift of prophecy—just as those who were rebaptized by Paul had done (Acts 19:6). No specifics are recorded as to what the prophecies were except that Joseph stated he had prophesied concerning events involving the Church that had not yet come to pass. Joseph recorded that their minds were enlightened as never before, and they were able to understand the true meaning and intention of the scriptures—including what he designated (but did not identify) as their "mysterious passages" (HC 1:43). However, they had to keep the circumstances of their baptisms secret due to the spirit of persecution in the area. John the Baptist also told Joseph and Oliver at this time that Joseph was to be called the First Elder of the Church and Oliver the Second Elder.

17   HC 1:44, 51.

And again, what do we hear? Glad tidings from Cumorah, Moroni, an angel from heaven, declaring the fulfillment of the prophets—the book to be revealed.

Peter, James, and John restored the Melchizedek Priesthood to Joseph Smith and Oliver Cowdery in 1829.

A voice of the Lord in the wilderness of Fayette, Seneca county, declaring the three witnesses to bear record of the book. The voice of Michael on the banks of the Susquehanna, detecting the devil when he appeared as an angel of light! *The voice of Peter, James, and John in the wilderness between Harmony, Susquehanna county, and Colesville, Broome county, on the Susquehanna river, declaring themselves as possessing the keys of the kingdom, and of the dispensation of the fulness of times.*[18]

This letter, although written in 1842, records an earlier sequence of events that occurred during the Restoration, including the restoration of the Melchizedek Priesthood by Peter, James, and John. The Lord also refers to this restoration in a revelation given to the Prophet in 1830 wherein He declared that He had sent Peter, James, and John to ordain and confirm Joseph and Oliver as "apostles, and special witnesses of [His] name."[19]

Additional information pertaining to when the Melchizedek Priesthood was restored is contained in Section 18 of the Doctrine and Covenants, which was revealed in June of 1829. In that section, the Lord called Oliver Cowdery and David Whitmer as Apostles, as He did Paul of old, and commissioned them to seek out the first twelve Apostles of the latter days.[20]

---

18   D&C 128:20. Emphasis added.

19   D&C 27:12.

20   D&C 18:11, 37.

Taking all these references into account, it can be determined that the Melchizedek Priesthood was restored by Peter, James, and John sometime between May 15, 1829, and the end of June 1829,[21] thus completing the restoration of priesthood authority that had been lost during the Dark Ages.

Proselyting Helps

Baptism is required for entrance into the kingdom of God, but there is a caveat: it must be done by someone holding the proper authority.

- Proper priesthood authority has always been necessary for mankind to act in God's name.

- Priesthood authority cannot be usurped or purchased. It can only be conferred by one holding the proper authority himself.

- A man must hold the Priesthood in order to perform the ordinance of baptism.

- John the Baptist held the Aaronic Priesthood. This gave him the authority to baptize Jesus when He requested it.

- Nephi recounts five reasons for the Savior to be baptized: (1) to show His humility before the Father; (2) to show He is obedient to the Father and will keep His commandments; (3) to show that baptism is necessary prior to receiving the Holy Ghost; (4) To show mankind the path they need to follow to enter the Father's kingdom; (5) to invite all mankind to follow His example.

---

21   HC 1:40 ftnt et seq., for a lengthy discussion on determining the approximate date of the restoration of the Melchizedek Priesthood.

- John the Baptist restored the Aaronic Priesthood to Joseph Smith and Oliver Cowdery on May 15, 1829.

- Once Joseph and Oliver had received the Aaronic Priesthood and been baptized, they were able to baptize others.

- Joseph and Oliver received the Melchizedek Priesthood from Peter, James, and John sometime between May 15 and June 30, 1829.

- Once Joseph and Oliver had received the Melchizedek Priesthood, they were able to bestow the gift of the Holy Ghost and confer priesthood authority on other righteous men.

The return of priesthood authority is a powerful evidence of the Restoration. In the LDS Church, worthy young men are given the Aaronic Priesthood at the age of twelve, and can receive the Melchizedek Priesthood as early as eighteen. Males who hold priesthood authority, however, have the responsibility to exercise it in righteousness.

Explaining the requirement of proper priesthood authority and the example of Christ's baptism by immersion can help nonmembers understand why they must be baptized again to become members of the LDS Church, even though they may have been baptized previously in another church. This doctrine can also be used to teach nonmembers why they are required to be baptized, verses simply "accepting Christ."

The Covenant of Abraham

God renewed his commitment to Israel when the covenant of Abraham was returned to the earth in 1836. This evidence of the Restoration resulted in the blessings of the Abrahamic covenant again being made available to mankind.

Abram (whose name was later changed to Abraham by the Lord) lived circa 2000 B.C. The genealogical record in the Old Testament follows the incident at the tower of Babel and lists Abraham's father as Terah. The scriptures also note that he had two brothers: Nahor and Haran. Haran died leaving a son named Lot, Abraham's nephew. Abraham married the beautiful Sarai, but she was barren. The scriptures note that the family moved from Ur of the Chaldees to the land of Haran. The emphasis in the scriptures then shifts from Abraham's temporal existence to his dealings with the Lord.

The Lord commanded Abraham to leave his father's kindred and move from Haran, promising to give him and his seed (which He described as being as numerous as the stars of heaven) the land of Canaan. The Lord then declared that the covenant He had made with Abraham was an everlasting covenant, that Abraham and his seed would be His chosen people, and

The covenant God made with Abraham was an everlasting covenant.

that He would be a God unto Abraham and to his seed after him.[1] When the Lord finished outlining the terms and conditions of His arrangement with Abraham, and Abraham had accepted those terms, their agreement became known as the "Abrahamic covenant." The covenant is important because of the following issues:

- It defines the basis of our relationship with God.

- It identifies God's chosen people.

- It is evidence of God's promises to His chosen people and the blessings He has in store for them.

- It grants God's priesthood authority to mankind so that the work of salvation can be accomplished for His children.

- It outlines our responsibilities and opportunities once we accept its parameters.

We sometimes define the word *covenant* as a contract between two parties, but with regard to the covenant of Abraham, the definition requires modification. When God made His covenant with Abraham and his progeny, He alone established its terms, conditions, and blessings. There were no negotiations—mankind could merely accept or reject the terms and conditions of the covenant.

God made this covenant with Abraham when Abraham was ninety-nine years old,[2] and He promised He would never break nor revoke it. It is composed of three parts. The first is absolute and unconditional, but the others, though absolute, are conditionally based on the righteousness of

---

1   Genesis 17:1-8.

2   Genesis 17:1.

God's chosen people. If they sin (collectively or individually) and become unworthy, they will still remain God's chosen people, but the right to the blessings of the covenant will be rescinded until He either restores it to them or casts them off forever.

These three parts of the covenant require further examination:

The covenant of Abraham has three parts.

Part One   Abraham was promised he would have "seed" (progeny), and his seed would forever be designated as the Lord's *chosen* people. God chose them and He will never reject them.

Part Two   The chosen people will be blessed with a *promised land.* For Abraham, the promised land was Canaan,[3] and Canaan remained the promised land throughout the generations of Isaac and Jacob (Jacob's name was later changed to Israel by the Lord). Jacob, or Israel, had twelve sons, collectively known as the twelve tribes of Israel, or the children of Israel. After Moses led the tribes out of Egypt, they returned to the promised land of Canaan and divided it among themselves. Later, after the ten tribes were lost, Judah (and members of the other tribes residing within her boundaries—then known as the Southern Kingdom) retained the general area of Canaan, including Jerusalem. This area later became generally known as Palestine. A branch of the tribe of Joseph (comprising Ephraim and Manasseh) residing in the area circa 600 B.C. was led out of Jerusalem and given the Western Hemisphere as its promised land.[4]

---

3   Genesis 17:8.

4   1 Nephi 2:20; 3 Nephi 20:13–14.

Part Three   The chosen people will be given the *priesthood.*[5] This priesthood was originally given to Adam by God. It was then passed down through the ages by ordination until it was given to Abraham,[6] and through Abraham, it became part of the Abrahamic covenant. All of the blessings of the gospel of salvation, "even of life eternal," come through the priesthood.[7] Without the priesthood, eternal life (i.e., living in the presence of God) cannot be realized.

All Abraham had to do to receive the blessings of this irrevocable covenant was to accept it and comply with its conditions. The sign of his acceptance (and the acceptance of all males after him until the time of Christ) was circumcision.

Acceptance of the covenant of Abraham requires that the individual accept two responsibilities. First, the recipient must walk uprightly before | Acceptance of the Abrahamic Covenant includes two responsibilities.

God and be "perfect."[8] God clearly stated His intentions when He said, "And we [the Creators] will prove them herewith, to see if they will do all things whatsoever the Lord their God shall command them."[9] In other words, the Lord is saying, "walk before me, and be thou perfect."[10] This same requirement was reiterated by the Savior during His ministry when He gave the Sermon on the Mount: "Be ye therefore perfect, even as your Father which is in heaven is perfect."[11]

Second, the recipient must offer the gospel of salvation

---

5   Abraham 1:4; 2:11.

6   Abraham 1:3; D&C 84:14–16.

7   Abraham 2:11.

8   Genesis 17:1.

9   Abraham 3:25.

10   Genesis 17:1.

11   Matthew 5:48.

to the world.[12] Those under the Abrahamic covenant are required to "testify and warn the people." This responsibility is required because the gospel, i.e., the plan of salvation, is the plan that must be followed if mankind is to regain God's presence. Once the covenant has been accepted, "it becometh every man who has been warned to warn his neighbor."[13] The Lord's chosen people have the responsibility to take the gospel to "all nations, kindreds, tongues and people,"[14] with the result that "he that believeth and is baptized shall be saved; but he that believeth not shall be damned"[15] and "left without excuse." The sins of those individuals will then be "upon their own heads."[16]

From Abraham, the covenant passed first to Isaac[17] and then to Jacob (aka Israel).[18] Thereafter, it went to Jacob's twelve sons, collectively known as the twelve tribes (or house) of Israel.[19] However, *anyone* can become one of God's chosen people and share in the blessings of the covenant of Abraham if he or she is willing to accept and live the gospel.[20]

Anyone can become one of God's chosen people.

On April 3, 1836, the prophet Elias appeared to Joseph Smith and Oliver Cowdery in the Kirtland Temple and committed to them the keys to the dispensation of the gospel (or covenant) of Abraham, thus restoring the covenant of Abraham to the earth. As noted, acceptance of the gospel (evidenced by repentance, baptism, confirmation, and obedience to God's command-

The prophet Elias restored the covenant of Abraham to the earth in 1836.

---

12   See Abraham 2:11.

13   D&C 88:81.

14   D&C 42:58.

15   Mark 16:16.

16   D&C 88:82.

17   Genesis 17:21.

18   Genesis 32:28.

19   Exodus 6:7–8; Deuteronomy 4:20.

20   2 Nephi 30:1–2.

ments) automatically makes an individual part of Israel's lineage.[21]

With the establishment of Christ's church during His ministry, the sign of the Abrahamic covenant was changed from circumcision to baptism. When the covenant was restored during the Restoration, the Lord renewed His commitment to Israel and now, through the work of the Prophet Joseph Smith, the blessings of the covenant are once again available to all mankind.

Proselyting Helps

A covenant is a contract between two parties. God made an everlasting covenant with the prophet Abraham: Abraham and his seed would be God's chosen people and receive His blessings; in return, He would be their God, and they would covenant to obey his commandments.

- The covenant of Abraham defines the basis of our relationship with God, identifies God's chosen people, provides evidence of God's promises to His chosen people and the blessings He has in store for them, grants God's priesthood authority to mankind, and outlines the responsibilities of those who accept it.

- The blessings of the covenant comprise three parts: (1) Abraham's vast progeny would be designated as God's chosen people. (2) The chosen people would be blessed with a promised land. (3) They would be given the priesthood.

- Acceptance of the Abrahamic covenant requires the individual to accept two responsibilities: (1) The recipient must walk uprightly before God and be "perfect." (2)

---

21   Romans 8:14-17; Galatians 4:4-7.

The recipient must offer the gospel of salvation to the world.

• Acceptance of the gospel is evidenced by repentance, baptism, confirmation, and obedience to God's commandments, and automatically makes an individual part of Israel's lineage.

• The sign of the Abrahamic covenant was changed from circumcision to baptism at the time of Christ's ministry.

• All the blessings of the gospel of salvation, including eternal life, come through the priesthood.

• The prophet Elias appeared to Joseph Smith and Oliver Cowdery on April 3, 1836, and committed to them the keys of the dispensation of the gospel (or the covenant) of Abraham.

The return of the covenant of Abraham to the earth is yet another evidence of the Restoration. Anyone can become a member of the house of Israel—one of God's chosen people—and share in the blessings of the Abrahamic covenant if he or she is willing to accept the gospel. Those who accept the gospel and bend their will to the will of the Father will receive eternal life in the Father's kingdom and become joint-heirs with Jesus Christ. Gaining a greater appreciation for the blessings the Father has in store for us tends to increase our desire to share those blessings with our family and friends. That, in turn, can help us overcome our fear of talking to them about the gospel.

*Thus saith the Lord God; Behold, I will take
the children of Israel from among the heathen,
whither they be gone, and will gather them on
every side, and bring them into their own land.*

Ezekiel 37:21

The Gathering

The gathering is the most visible evidence of
the Restoration. It not only encompasses the
gathering of the twelve tribes of Israel to their
promised lands, but a general gathering of all
people to the gospel of Jesus Christ.

Israel's twelve sons were named Reuben, Simeon, Levi,
Judah, Zebulun, Issachar, Dan, Gad, Asher, Naphtali, Joseph, and Benjamin. As noted in the previous chapter,
these twelve sons and their descendants became known as
the house of Israel, the twelve tribes of Israel, or just Israel.
God chose these tribes to be His people, for as He said to
Moses, "Ye shall be a peculiar treasure unto me above all
people."[1] Isaiah confirmed this unique selection when he
declared, "Thus saith the Lord that created thee, O Jacob,
and he that formed thee, O Israel, . . . I am the Lord, your
Holy One, the creator of Israel."[2]

---

1   Exodus 19:5; Torah 526. In the Torah translation, the same verse reads:
      "You shall be My treasured possession among all the peoples."

2   Isaiah 43:1, 15.

For the most part, the tribes of Israel were united as a nation until the end of the reign of King Solomon. After his death, however, the nation divided and the divisions became known as the Northern and Southern Kingdoms. The Northern Kingdom was also called the Kingdom of Israel, and was inhabited by the tribes of Reuben, Simeon, Zebulun, Issachar, Dan, Gad, Asher, Naphtali, Levi, Joseph, and large parts of Benjamin. These tribes were conquered by Assyria circa 721 B.C., after the people had become wicked and rejected the Lord. After the Assyrians carried them off, they subsequently became "lost."[3] They have since been described as *the lost ten tribes* or *the lost tribes of Israel.*[4]

Essentially, ten of the twelve tribes have become lost through the ages.

After the destruction of the Northern Kingdom, the Southern Kingdom eventually became known as Israel. It was also known as the Kingdom of Judah because Judah was the only whole tribe left that lived there (parts of Benjamin, Levi, Joseph, and individual members of other tribes also resided in Judah).

Because of the predominance of the tribe of Judah in the Southern Kingdom, those who belonged to other tribes also became known politically as "Jews." An example of this is recorded by the prophet Lehi. He was a descendant of Joseph,[5] yet his son Nephi records that the remnants of his seed were Jews (not by lineage, but by nationality).[6] A second example is found in the book of Esther. Mordecai, the man who raised Esther, was introduced in the text as "a certain Jew," yet he was of the tribe of Benjamin.[7] Eventually (and especially today), the terms "Jews" and "Israel" became synonymous. This amalgamation of terminology is the predominant reason for the apostate belief that

3   2 Kings 17:6; 18:11-12.

4   See 2 Nephi 29:13; 3 Nephi 17:4; 21:26.

5   1 Nephi 5:14.

6   2 Nephi 30:4.

7   Esther 2:5.

the doctrine of the gathering concerns only the Jews. The Jews themselves have adopted this amalgamation of their name, to the extent that they project it not only forward, but backward (at least as far back as the Exodus since one commentary on the Torah states that the purpose of the Passover Seder is to "[rehearse] the Exodus and the birth of the *Jewish* [rather than Israelite] people").[8]

As the Lord told Nephi, however, "Know ye not that there are more nations than one?"[9] The fact remains that twelve tribes were scattered and twelve tribes must be gathered!

No church can claim to be God's true church without teaching the doctrine of the gathering correctly. Furthermore, no church can claim to be true unless it receives authority from God to gather His people.

The gathering confirms the fact that the Lord's gospel has been restored and His Second Coming is nigh.

The gathering is one of the greatest signs the people of the earth will receive to confirm the fact that the Savior's ancient gospel has been restored and that the Second Coming of Jesus Christ is nigh at hand. It is also one of the doctrines that creates the most confusion in the Christian and Jewish worlds. While the gathering is defined as the physical return of the people of Israel to their promised lands, it also denotes the gathering of all the people of the world—Jew and Gentile—to the Lord and His gospel.[10]

In the strict sense, a Gentile is someone who has descended from Japheth,[11] the oldest son of Noah.[12] However, the term Gentile is used in multiple ways throughout the scriptures to describe:

---

8   Torah 431. Emphasis added.

9   2 Nephi 29:7.

10   Isaiah 49:6.

11   Moses 8:12; Inspired Version, Genesis 7:85.

12   Genesis 10:1–5.

1. those nations into which Israel was scattered,

2. the heathen,

3. the unrighteous,

4. those not of Israel, and

5. non-Jews.[13]

For the purpose of gathering the people of the earth to the gospel, the term Gentile would include all of the above, as well as those who are neither Israelite nor Gentile: i.e., those of the seed of Abraham who are descendants of Ishmael and Abraham's other children; and those who descended from Noah's son, Ham. Even though these races are not classified as Gentiles in other situations and are not specifically referred to in the gathering scriptures, Isaiah makes it clear that the Lord's gospel is to be offered to *all* the people of the earth.[14] Therefore, this general gathering of the repentant to the gospel is inclusive of all peoples.[15]

On April 3, 1836, Moses appeared to Joseph Smith and Oliver Cowdery in the Kirtland Temple and restored "the keys of the gathering

> Moses restored the keys to the gathering of Israel on April 3, 1836.

of Israel from the four parts of the earth, and the leading of the ten tribes from the land of the north."[16] In actuality, however, the scriptures make it clear that *five* distinct groups of people must be gathered in preparation for the Second Coming of the Lord: Judah, the ten lost tribes, the Lamanites (Manasseh), Ephraim, and the Gentiles (which would include the Arabs and those of African descent).

Judah

Judah is to be gathered to Jerusalem, a scriptural syn-

---

13 SC 252, ftnt 3.

14 Isaiah 49:6.

15 2 Nephi 30:1–2; Jacob 5.

16 D&C 110:11.

onym for the promised land which is now encompassed within the State of Israel.[17] In the process of obeying the Lord's commandment to gather Israel, Joseph Smith commissioned Orson Hyde to go to the land of Palestine and dedicate that land for the gathering of the tribe of Judah. There, on October 24, 1841, Orson Hyde gave that dedicatory prayer. On his return trip to Nauvoo, Elder Hyde wrote to Joseph indicating that the gathering spirit was moving upon the Jews.[18] However, perhaps even more interesting than Elder Hyde's comment is the report Golda Meir made in her autobiography regarding the spirit of gathering:

A great deal has already been written—and much more will certainly be written in the future—about the Zionist movement, and most people by now have at least some notion of what the word 'Zionism' means and that it has to do with the return of the Jewish people to the land of their forefathers– the Land of Israel, as it is called in Hebrew. But perhaps even today not everyone realizes that *this remarkable movement sprang up spontaneously, and more or less simultaneously, in various parts of Europe toward the end of the nineteenth century.* It was like a drama that was being enacted in different ways on different stages in different languages but that dealt with the same theme everywhere: that the so-called Jewish problem (of course, it was really a Christian problem) was basically the result of Jewish homelessness and that it could not, and would not, be solved unless and until the Jews had a land of their

> The tribe of Judah is gathering to Israel, its promised land.

17   SC, Chapter 5.

18   HC 4:459.

own again. Obviously, this land could only be Zion, the land from which the Jews had been exiled 2,000 years before but which had remained the spiritual center of Jewry throughout the centuries and which, when I was a little girl in Pinsk and up to the end of World War I, was a desolate and neglected province of the Ottoman Empire called Palestine.[19]

Although Golda Meir probably did not understand the origins of the movement she described, and had undoubtedly never heard of Orson Hyde, her description of the results of Elder Hyde's prayer and the movement of the spirit of gathering on the descendants of Judah could not have been more eloquently described.

The Ten Lost Tribes

Since no one knows where the lost ten tribes reside as a unit, any reference to their location is speculative. And while individual members of any given tribe may occasionally be located and brought within the gospel covenant, the lost tribes as a whole will not be found until the Second Coming. The following information is all we know about them:

> When the lost ten tribes are found, they will be gathered to Zion.

1. They are described as being located in the "north" countries.[20]

2. The Savior went to the lost tribes after His resurrection and ministered to them.[21]

3. In the last days, the "work of the Father" will commence

---

19   GM 23. Emphasis added.

20   Jeremiah 16:14-15; D&C 110:11; 133:26.

21   3 Nephi 17:4.

among them (this work will probably be independent of the Church since the tribes are currently "lost").[22]

4. Joseph Smith stated that John the Revelator was preaching among them.[23]

5. Their scriptural records will eventually be available to the other tribes.[24]

6. They will be gathered out from the wicked at the destruction of the devil's kingdom.[25]

7. They will be gathered from the north country[26] to join the other tribes of Israel (Judah and Joseph).[27]

8. At their return, a great highway will be cast up (perhaps not an actual highway, but the symbolic means by which the Lord will gather them).[28]

9. Their former enemies "shall become a prey unto them."[29]

10. They will eventually receive all of the blessings of the covenant of Abraham in Zion; the gospel will be preached to them and they will receive their glory.[30]

11. They will bring their treasures to the tribe of Ephraim in Zion, "And there shall they fall down and be crowned with glory, even in Zion, by the hands of the servants of the Lord, even the children of Ephraim."[31]

12. Songs of everlasting joy will be sung at their return.[32]

---

22 3 Nephi 21:26.

23 HC 1:176 ftnt.

24 2 Nephi 29:13.

25 Isaiah 13:5, 14–22.

26 SC 252, ftnt 5.

27 Jeremiah 3:18; Zechariah 2:6; Articles of Faith 1:10.

28 Isaiah 11:16; 35:8–10; D&C 133:27.

29 D&C 133:28.

30 Isaiah 35:8–10; 3 Nephi 21:26; D&C 133:28–32.

31 D&C 133:32; Isaiah 60:8–12.

32 D&C 133:33; SC 252, ftnt 6.

The Lamanites

Even though the Lamanites are described in the allegory of the vineyard found in Chapter 5 of the book | Manasseh (the Lamanites) will be gathered to the gospel.

of Jacob as an unrighteous and wild branch of the tame olive tree, the Book of Mormon promises that they will be preserved and their days prolonged until the time they are gathered[33] and grafted back into the olive tree as a natural branch.[34] The desire to gather the Lamanites to the restored gospel of Jesus Christ commenced soon after the organization of the Church in 1830. During a conference of the Church on September 26, 1830, several brethren expressed the desire to serve a mission to the Lamanites. Joseph inquired of the Lord concerning this, and the revelation contained in Section 32 of the Doctrine and Covenants was the result. Missionary work among the Lamanites commenced immediately thereafter, since one of the purposes of the Book of Mormon is to convince the Lamanites of the truthfulness of the gospel.[35] Through the Book of Mormon, they will come to realize that they are of the house of Israel[36] and that making the gospel available to them fulfills prophecy.[37] Subsequent to this early mission, many Lamanites have been called to repentance, have acknowledged the Bible as the word of God, and have acknowledged the truthfulness of the Book of Mormon. Many have accepted Christ and have once again been brought under the covenant of Abraham.[38] Upon acceptance of these blessings, their civilization will flourish in the wilderness and "blossom as the rose."[39]

The impressive number of temples the church has built throughout Central and South America in recent years to

---

33 Helaman 15:11-16.

34 1 Nephi 15:16.

35 Mormon 5:12-15.

36 2 Nephi 30:3-6.

37 1 Nephi 15:14; Alma 9:16-17; 3 Nephi 20-21.

38 Mormon 7:1-10.

39 D&C 49:24; 3 Nephi 5:21-26; SC 252, ftnt 7.

accommodate the growing number of active converts in those areas suggests that the gathering of the Lamanites is well underway.

Ephraim

The Lord's ancient prophets prophesied that almost immediately after the restoration of the gospel, | The tribe of Ephraim will also be gathered to Zion.

missionaries would be sent to the world to declare its glad tidings.[40] They would be sent to the nations of the world and the isles of the sea to gather not only a scattered Ephraim,[41] but all Israel from the four corners of the earth.[42] Just as the spirit of gathering moved upon the tribe of Judah after Orson Hyde's dedicatory prayer,[43] so also did it move upon those (predominately of Ephraim) who heard the gospel of salvation preached in Great Britain during the early years of the Church—in spite of the fact that Joseph Smith had instructed those leaving for the British mission *not* to teach the gathering until the gospel had been established there. But the Spirit clearly manifested otherwise.[44] The keys of the gathering had been restored[45] and a gathering spirit moved upon mankind, regardless of whether the missionaries taught it or not.

No sooner were the people baptized than they were seized with a desire to gather with the main body of the Church. "I | The spirit of gathering moved strongly upon early converts to the Church.

find it is difficult to keep anything from the Saints," writes Elder Taylor in his journal from this period, "for the Spirit of God re-

---

40 Isaiah 18; Jeremiah 16:14-16.
41 Zechariah 10:6-12.
42 Matthew 24:31; 1 Nephi 22:25; D&C 133:7-8; SC 252, ftnt 8.
43 HC 4:456-457.
44 HC 2:492.
45 D&C 110:11.

veals it to them. . . . Some time ago Sister Mitchell dreamed that she, her husband and a number of others were on board a vessel, and that there were other vessels, loaded with Saints, going somewhere. She felt very happy and was rejoicing in the Lord." Another sister, Elder Taylor informs us, had a similar dream, and was informed that all the Saints were going. Neither of these sisters nor any of the Saints at that time, knew anything about the principle of gathering, yet all were anxious to leave their homes, their kindred and the associations of a lifetime, to join the main body of the Church in a distant land, the members of which were total strangers to them. The same spirit has rested upon the people in every nation where the Gospel has been received. There has been little need of preaching the gathering, the people as a rule have had to be restrained rather than encouraged in the matter of gathering to Zion and her stakes.[46]

Needless to say, the gathering from the British Mission moved forward rapidly because "the Spirit of the Lord Jesus Christ is a gathering spirit."[47]

In compliance with the covenant of Abraham, during the Restoration the Lord commanded that converts to The Church of Jesus Christ of Latter-day Saints be gathered to a "promised land."[48] Consequently, in June of 1831, the Lord told Joseph Smith and Sidney Rigdon to leave their homes and go to the land of Missouri.[49] They were in-

46   HC 2:XXVII.
47   HC 6:12.
48   D&C 29:7-8.
49   D&C 52:3.

structed to hold a conference there, on the land the Lord would consecrate unto His people—a remnant of Jacob—"those who are heirs according to the covenant."[50] Furthermore, the scriptures note that the sacred city of Zion spoken of by David in Psalm 102 would be built upon the land of America,[51] where the "ransomed of the Lord" could "return and come to Zion with songs and everlasting joy upon their heads."[52] Although Zion was *not* redeemed in Joseph's time due to the transgressions of the early Saints[53] and the heavy persecution they encountered, it will yet be redeemed in the Lord's due time.[54]

Today, Missionaries are sent to gather Ephraim and the remnants of the other tribes of Israel from among | Today, the Saints gather to the stakes of the Church.

the people of the earth in "all the lands whither [the Lord has] driven them,"[55] so that they may receive the word of God and come to the ensign (gospel) that God has established in the latter days.[56] Obstacles will be removed to allow the gathering to take place, for as the Lord said in Ezekiel, "I will bring you out from the people, and will gather you out of the countries wherein ye are scattered, with a mighty hand, and with a stretched out arm, and with fury poured out. . . . I will cause you to pass under the rod [of judgment], and I will bring you into the bond of the covenant."[57]

Until the Lord redeems Zion and gathers the Saints (preparatory to His return to the New Jerusalem), converts are to be gathered where "the Lord shall locate a stake of

---

50   D&C 52:2; D&C 57:1.
51   HC 1:315.
52   Isaiah 35:10.
53   D&C 105:9.
54   D&C 136:18.
55   Jeremiah 16:14–16; Isaiah 18.
56   Isaiah 11:11–12; Daniel 2.
57   Ezekiel 20:34, 37.

Zion."[58] These stakes are to be appointed in "the regions round about" as they shall be manifested unto the Lord's servants, and will be created as "curtains or the strength of Zion."[59]

The Gentiles

(Including the Arabs and Those of African Descent)

The title page of the Book of Mormon states that the book's message (i.e., the gospel) is to be brought forth

| The Gentiles will be gathered through missionary work.

not only for the remnant of the house of Israel, but also for the "convincing of the Jew and Gentile that Jesus is the Christ." There are nowhere near the number of scriptural references concerning the gathering of the Gentiles (and none specifically relating to the Arabs and those of African descent) as there are concerning the gathering of Israel, but there is a sufficient number to make two things clear: (a) the Gentiles, including the Arabs and those of African descent, will have the gospel taught to them and will have the opportunity to gather and become heirs according to the covenant, and (b) once they repent and become heirs according to the covenant, they will be included in all of the general gathering scriptures.

During His visit to the Western Hemisphere, the Lord stated that there were many "not of this land" who had not yet heard His voice. He declared that His words would "be manifested unto the Gentiles"[60] and that in the latter days, they would receive the truth.[61] Many would reject the gospel,[62] but in the Doctrine and Covenants, the Lord reaffirmed that the missionaries would be prepared to extend the gospel to both Gentile and Jew, as many as would

---

58   D&C 109:39; 136:10.
59   D&C 101:21; 115:18.
60   3 Nephi 16:1–4.
61   3 Nephi 16:7.
62   3 Nephi 16:10.

believe.[63] Finally, Paul wrote to the Romans describing the Gentiles as a "wild olive tree" that when grafted in among the branches of the good olive tree, could partake of the "root and fatness of the [natural] tree"[64] and become heirs to the covenant of Abraham.

The sign of the gathering, both the specific gathering and the general gathering, has been preached by almost all of God's prophets from earliest times. Enoch rejoiced in the knowledge of Zion (the New Jerusalem) and those who would gather to it[65] and Moses, after prophesying of the diaspora, declared:

> But if from thence thou shalt seek the Lord thy God, thou shalt find him, if thou seek him with all thy heart and with all thy soul.
>
> When thou art in tribulation, and all these things are come upon thee, *even in the latter days,* if thou turn to the Lord thy God, and shalt be obedient unto his voice;
>
> (For the Lord thy God is a merciful God;) he will not forsake thee, neither destroy thee, nor forget the covenant of thy fathers which he sware unto them.[66]

Isaiah spoke of the gathering in many chapters of his book.[67] Jeremiah spoke of it in five of his chapters[68] and Ezekiel in five of his.[69] It is

> The gathering was prophesied by almost all of God's ancient prophets.

---

63   D&C 18:26; 90:8.

64   Romans 11:16-26.

65   Moses 7:62.

66   Deuteronomy 4:29-31. Emphasis added.

67   Isaiah 2:2-3; 10:20-22; 11:11, 13; 13:2-4; 14:1-33; 30:18-25; 33:17-24; 40:27-31; 43:5-7; 49; 52:2-3, 6-7; 62.

68   Jeremiah 3:17-18; 23:3-8; 31; 32:37-44; 50:4-6.

69   Ezekiel 11:16-20; 20:34-38; 34:11-19; 36:16-38; 37:1-14, 16-22.

also mentioned in Hosea,[70] Amos,[71] Micah,[72] Zephaniah,[73] Zechariah,[74] and Joel.[75] Book of Mormon prophets also spoke of it,[76] and once the Restoration was complete, the Lord spoke of it repeatedly in the Doctrine and Covenants.[77]

John the Revelator was given a vision of a "little book," which symbolically represented the gathering. The Lord commanded John to eat the little book, but although it was sweet to his taste, it became bitter in his belly[78] when he saw those who would not repent and come unto Christ. However, it was sweet when he saw the culmination of the gathering and the reuniting of the great cities of Jerusalem, Enoch, and the New Jerusalem at the Lord's Second Coming.[79]

The sign of the gathering, probably the most visible evidence of the Restoration to date, is ongoing. It commenced with the restoration of the gospel and will accelerate as the Lord's advent becomes imminent. The scriptures state that angels will assist men in the final gathering[80] and it will not be complete until all the righteous have been gathered into the Savior's kingdom.

> Therefore, behold, the days come, saith the Lord, that they shall no more say, The Lord liveth, which brought up the children of Israel out of the land of Egypt;
>
> But, The Lord liveth, which brought up and which led the seed of the house of

---

70 Hosea 1:10-11.
71 Amos 9:11-15.
72 Micah 2:12; 4:6-7; 5:3.
73 Zephaniah 3:14-21.
74 Zechariah 8:4-7, 12-13; 10:6-12; 14:10-11.
75 Joel 2:32.
76 1 Nephi 15:14; 22:11-12; 3 Nephi 5:24-26; 20; 21.
77 See D&C Index, s.v. Gather, Gathering.
78 Revelation 10:9-10; D&C 77:14.
79 Revelation 21.
80 Joseph Smith - Matthew 1:37.

Israel out of the north country, and from all countries whither I had driven them; and they shall dwell in their own land.[81]

Proselyting Helps

As the Second Coming approaches, the gathering of the tribes of Israel to their promised lands, and the gathering of people in general to the gospel, will continue. This visible sign is another powerful evidence of the Restoration.

- The gathering was prophesied by almost all of God's ancient prophets.

- Moses restored the keys to the gathering of Israel to Joseph Smith and Oliver Cowdery in the Kirtland Temple on April 3, 1836.

- No church can be true unless it receives its authority from God to gather His people.

- The gathering is the sign that the Lord's gospel has been restored and His Second Coming is nigh.

- The tribes of Israel were essentially united up to the end of King Solomon's reign, but after his death the nations divided. Approximately ten of the tribes became known as the Northern Kingdom, or Kingdom of Israel. These tribes were conquered by Assyria, carried off, and subsequently became lost. They will be gathered to Zion sometime around the Second Coming.

- After the destruction of the Northern Kingdom, the Southern Kingdom became known as Israel, or the Kingdom of Judah since Judah was the only whole tribe living

---

81   Jeremiah 23:7-8; see also 16:14-16.

there. Politically, all of its citizens were called "Jews." Today, the tribe of Judah is gathering back to Israel.

- The tribe of Manasseh (the Lamanites) is being gathered to the gospel.

- The tribe of Ephraim will be gathered to its promised land of Zion.

- The spirit of gathering moved strongly upon the early converts to the Church. They gathered to and moved with the Church until it settled in the Salt Lake Valley. Today, the Saints gather to the stakes of Zion, awaiting the time when the Lord will redeem their promised land.

- Through missionary efforts, the Gentiles will have the opportunity to be gathered to the gospel.

The Lord will continue to gather His people for the last time as the Second Coming approaches. "For behold, the field is white, already to harvest; and it is the eleventh hour, and the last time I shall call laborers into my vineyard" (D&C 33:3). Member missionaries and full-time missionaries alike have the unique opportunity to assist the Lord in this work. Individuals who are introduced to the gospel by a friend are far more likely to accept the gospel. The people around us are, in fact, aware of who and what we are, and many are waiting for us to offer them the opportunity to learn more.

And it shall come to pass in the last days,
that . . . many people shall go and say, Come
ye, and let us go up to the mountain of the
Lord . . . for out of Zion shall go forth the law,
and the word of the Lord from Jerusalem.

Isaiah 2:2–3

$\mathcal{J}$he $\mathcal{P}$romised $\mathcal{L}$and

One of the blessings inherent in the covenant of Abraham is a promised land. Anciently, the Lord gave the tribes of Israel a promised land on the Eastern Hemisphere. In the dispensation of the fullness of times, He designated a promised land for the Latter-day Saints on the Western Hemisphere—tangible evidence of the Restoration.

Prophecy tells us there are two great cities that will be established in the latter days: one is the city of Jerusalem; the other is the city of Zion.[1] The Lord prophesied of Zion's future existence when He visited the Western Hemi-

> Two great cities will be established in the latter days.

---

1   SC 182. Although there are more than seventeen different uses of the term "Zion" in the scriptures that describe such things as a mountain (Deuteronomy 4:48), a doctrine (1 Nephi 13: 36–37; D&C 133:9), a country, (HC 6:318–319), a people (D&C 97:21), or the location of a specific city (2 Samuel 5:7; Moses 7:19), this chapter will focus on the latter-day promised land of Zion that the Lord provided—and will yet provide—for the members of His restored church.

sphere after His resurrection. He declared that it would be established "in this land," meaning America,[2] and that both the "remnant of Jacob" and the Gentiles would assist in its construction.[3]

Enoch viewed the establishment of Zion after he had been translated into heaven,[4] and Ether saw this promised land in vision hundreds of years before the time of Christ. He called it a "New Jerusalem" and stated that it would be established "upon this land," meaning the Western Hemisphere.[5] But it was Isaiah and Micah, two of the Lord's ancient biblical prophets, who foresaw and described its glory. It would be one of the two world capitals from which the Lord would govern during the millennium: "for out of Zion shall go forth the law," they declared, or as Joel metaphorically stated, "the Lord also shall roar out of Zion."[6]

The City of Zion

The tenth article of faith states, "We believe in the literal gathering of Israel and in the restoration of the Ten Tribes; *that Zion (the New Jerusalem) will be built upon the American continent*; that Christ will reign personally upon the earth; and, that the earth will be renewed and receive its paradisiacal glory."[7]

For the gospel to be true (and not just another reformation of Christianity), its restoration had to include the assurance of a promised land. Not the *old* promised land, which was reserved for the gathering and restoration of Judah, but a *new* promised land where a gathering place for all the tribes of Israel *except* Judah would be established.

The location of the New Jerusalem (the city of Zion, or just "Zion") has now been identified, but the Lord slowly

2   3 Nephi 20:22.

3   3 Nephi 21:22-23.

4   Moses 7:62.

5   Ether 13:4-6.

6   Isaiah 2:3; Micah 4:2; Joel 3:16.

7   Articles of Faith 1:10. Emphasis added.

led the early members of the Church through the following step-by-step process, building their anticipation, before He revealed the city's exact location:

September 1830: The Lord revealed the existence of a promised land when He said, "No man knoweth where the city Zion shall be built, but it shall be given hereafter. Behold, I say unto you that it shall be on the borders by the Lamanites."[8]

February 1831: The Lord commanded the elders of the Church to move westward from Kirtland, Ohio, building up His church in every region, "Until the time shall come when it shall be revealed unto you from on high, when the city of the New Jerusalem shall be prepared, that ye may be my people and I will be your God."[9] The land for the city was to be purchased so that the Lord's covenant people could be gathered "in one" and the Lord could come to His temple.[10] But the Savior still did not tell the Saints *where* the city would be located, only that its exact location would be revealed in His own due time.[11]

March 1832: Section 48 of the Doctrine and Covenants was received, but the Lord still was not ready to reveal Zion's location. He promised to do so, however, after some of the brethren returned to Kirtland, Ohio, from the East. At that time, "certain men" would be appointed to know the place,[12] and the Lord would "hasten the city in its time" since its location at that point was in the hands of their enemies.[13]

---

8   D&C 28:9.
9   D&C 42:8-9.
10   D&C 42:35-36.
11   D&C 42:62.
12   D&C 48:5.
13   D&C 52:42-43.

June 1831: Pursuant to the Lord's command, the Prophet and others journeyed to Missouri to join another company of Saints.[14] Upon their arrival, Joseph pondered the great differences between what he called the "highly cultivated state of society in the east" and the "degradation, leanness of intellect, ferocity, and jealousy of the people that were nearly a century behind the times" in Missouri. While under the influence of these opinions, he cried to the Lord saying, "When will the wilderness blossom as the rose? When will Zion be built up in her glory, and where will Thy temple stand, unto which all nations shall come in the last days?"[15]

July 20, 1831: In what is now Section 57 of the Doctrine and Covenants, the Lord finally revealed the location of Zion to Joseph Smith.

Hearken, O ye elders of my church . . . who have assembled yourselves together, according to my commandments, in this land, which is the land of Missouri, which is the land which I have appointed and consecrated for the gathering of the saints.

> The location of Zion—Jackson County, Missouri—was revealed to Joseph in July 1831.

Wherefore, this is the *land of promise,* and the place for the city of Zion.

And thus saith the Lord your God, if you will receive wisdom here is wisdom. Behold, the place which is now called Independence is the *center place;* and a spot for the temple is lying westward, upon a lot which is not far from the courthouse.[16]

---

14   D&C 52:1-3.

15   HC 1:189.

16   D&C 57:1-3. Emphasis added.

While the Lord commonly calls this new city "Zion" in the Doctrine and Covenants,[17] He also calls it the New Jerusalem, "a land of peace, a city of refuge, a place of safety for the saints of the Most High God."[18] He notes that both the glory and the terror of the Lord will be in the city and the wicked will be afraid to go there.[19] The inhabitants of the city will be from every nation on earth and it will be the only city where the people will "not be at war one with another."[20] The righteous who gather to the city will sing "songs of everlasting joy" under the Lord's protection, and the wicked will refuse to go up against it, contending that "the inhabitants of Zion are terrible."[21]

Joseph Smith's astonishing declaration pertaining to the location of the city of Zion represented a radical departure from the apostate beliefs of his contemporaries. In his day, the term "Zion" was (and is) considered by the general Christian world to be a synonym for old Jerusalem and its environs. This is one of the major reasons for the misinterpretation of the scriptures pertaining to those cities in the latter days.

Zion Begins

The building up of the city of Zion was to begin from the original temple lot, a lot designated by the Lord as "Mount Zion."[22] However, the term symbolically refers to the exaltation or lifting up of Christ's gospel upon the earth, not to a physical description of the area (which is *not* mountainous).

The Saints proceeded to move into Missouri, acquiring territory for the establishment of Zion wherever they

---

17   D&C 45:67.
18   D&C 45:66.
19   D&C 45:67.
20   D&C 45:69.
21   D&C 45:70-71.
22   D&C 84:2-4.

settled. On August 1, 1831, on a site located twelve miles west of Independence in Kaw township, the first log was laid by Joseph Smith and members of the Colesville, New York, Branch of the Church for the first house in Zion.[23] On August 2, Sidney Rigdon was appointed to consecrate and dedicate the land for the establishment of Zion and the gathering of the Saints.[24] Before he started his prayer, he asked the Saints the following:

> Do you receive this land for the land of your inheritance with thankful hearts from the Lord?
> Answer from all: We do.
> Do you pledge yourselves to keep the law of God in this land which you never have kept in your own lands?
> We do.
> Do you pledge yourselves to see that others of your brethren who shall come hither do keep the laws of God?
> We do.[25]

Sidney then proceeded to give the prayer of dedication, after which he concluded: "I now pronounce this land consecrated and dedicated unto the Lord for a possession and inheritance for the Saints, and for all the faithful servants of the Lord to the remotest ages of time. In the name of Jesus Christ, having authority from Him. Amen.[26]

Sidney Rigdon dedicated the land of Zion in 1831.

Joseph noted in his journal that Sidney also commanded that they write a description of the land, and Joseph recorded the following:

---

23   HC 1:196.
24   D&C 58:57.
25   HC 1:196.
26   HC 1:196 & ftnt.

The country is unlike the timbered states of the East. As far as the eye can reach the beautiful rolling prairies lie spread out like a sea of meadows; and are decorated with a growth of flowers so gorgeous and grand as to exceed description; and nothing is more fruitful, or a richer stockholder in the blooming prairie than the honey bee. Only on the water courses is timber to be found. There in strips from one to three miles in width, and following faithfully the meandering of the streams, it grows in luxuriant forests. The forests are a mixture of oak, hickory, black walnut, elm, ash, cherry, honey locust, mulberry, coffee bean, hackberry, box elder, and bass wood; with the addition of cottonwood, butterwood, pecan, and soft and hard maple upon the bottoms. The shrubbery is beautiful, and consists in part of plums, grapes, crab apple, and persimmons.

The soil is rich and fertile; from three to ten feet deep, and generally composed of a rich black mould, intermingled with clay and sand. It yields in abundance, wheat, corn, sweet potatoes, cotton and many other common agricultural products. Horses, cattle and hogs, though of an inferior breed, are tolerably plentiful and seem nearly to raise themselves by grazing in the vast prairie range in summer, and feeding upon the bottoms in winter. The wild game is less plentiful of course where man has commenced the cultivation of the soil, than in the wild prairies. Buffalo, elk, deer, bear, wolves, beaver and many smaller animals here roam at pleasure. Turkeys, geese, swans, ducks, yea a variety of the feathered tribe, are among the rich abundance that grace the delightful regions of this goodly land—the heritage of the children of God.[27]

The climate in the area was mild nearly three quarters of the year, and in geographical terms of longitude and latitude, the land appeared to be equidistant between the Rocky Mountains and the Allegheny range. Joseph noted that the disadvantages of the area, however, were self-evident. As with any newly settled region, there was a "lack of mills and schools; together with the natural privations and inconveniences which the hand of industry, the refinement of society, and the polish of science, overcome."[28]

On August 3, 1831, Joseph Smith dedicated a specific spot for the temple.[29] According to his plat, however, the completed city would eventually have a total of twenty-four temples within its boundaries to ensure that the Lord's work would go forth.[30]

But Zion was not to be redeemed in Joseph's time. Severe persecution befell the Saints, persecution that culminated when Lilburn W. Boggs, then governor of Missouri, conspired with mobbers and other Church oppressors to issue his infamous *Extermination Order* expelling the Saints from the state.[31] Still, the Lord recognized the diligence and hard work of those early Saints, and He acknowledged the obstacles their enemies had placed in their way when He relieved them of the duty to build Zion at that time. He also severely cursed those who had hindered His work:

Persecution prevented the early Saints from inheriting their promised land.

---

27 HC 1:197.
28 HC 1:197–198.
29 HC 1:199.
30 HC 1:358–359.
31 HC 3:175.

Verily, verily, I say unto you, that when I give a commandment to any of the sons of men to do a work unto my name, and those sons of men go with all their might and with all they have to perform that work, and cease not their diligence, and their enemies come upon them and hinder them from performing that work, behold, it behooveth me to require that work no more at the hands of those sons of men, but to accept of their offerings.

And the iniquity and transgression of my holy laws and commandments I will visit upon the heads of those who hindered my work, unto the third and fourth generation, so long as they repent not, and hate me, saith the Lord God.

Therefore, for this cause have I accepted the offerings of those whom I commanded to build up a city and a house unto my name, in Jackson county, Missouri, and were hindered by their enemies, saith the Lord your God.

And I will answer judgment, wrath, and indignation, wailing, and anguish, and gnashing of teeth upon their heads, unto the third and fourth generation, so long as they repent not, and hate me, saith the Lord your God.[32]

Because they severely impeded the establishment of the Lord's holy city in the early days of the Restoration, God's wrath befell the people of Missouri and in time, "all the hardships the Missourians had inflected upon

---

32   D&C 124:49-52.

the Saints were . . . visited upon their heads, only more abundantly."[33]

While discussing his arrest and pending trial during his incarceration in Liberty Jail, Joseph Smith said to his attorney, A. W. Doniphan, "God's wrath hangs over Jackson County." He then prophesied that "The Lord of Hosts will sweep [Jackson County] with the besom of destruction. The fields and farms and houses will be destroyed, and only the chimneys will be left to mark the desolation."[34]

This remarkable prophecy was fulfilled through the devastation that befell Missouri and its people prior to and during the Civil War. Robert M. Stewart, Missouri's governor from 1847 to 1861, reported that several of Missouri's western counties were made desolate "and almost depopulated, from fear of a bandit horde" which had been and was committing "depredations—arson, theft, and foul murder" during the border warfare going on at the time.[35] General Sterling Price, who had previously had custody of the Prophet and had sorely mistreated him and other members of the Church, "destroyed upwards of 'ten million dollars worth of property,' a fair share of which belonged to his friends," during his Civil War skirmishes in Missouri.[36] And under Military Order No. 11 issued from Kansas City by General Thomas Ewing, the very people who had driven the Saints in Missouri from their homes and confiscated their personal property were themselves driven and expelled from their homes. "Their dwellings [were] burned, their farms laid waste, and the great bulk of their movable property handed over, without let or hindrance, to the Kansas 'jayhawkers.'"[37] During the first

---

33   HC 3:LXIII.

34   Janius F. Wells, "A Prophecy and Its Fulfillment," *Improvement Era*, November 1902, 9.

35   FM 14.

36   AC 360.

37   AC 351.

nineteen months of the Civil War (between April 20, 1861, and November 20, 1862), "over three hundred battles and skirmishes were fought within the limits of the State, . . . [and probably] half as many more" during the last two years,[38] with the result that much of the western border of Missouri was depopulated.[39]

The ancient prophet Mormon issued the following warning to those who would attempt to prevent the progress of God's work: "He that shall breathe out wrath and strifes against the work of the Lord, and against the covenant people of the Lord who are the house of Israel, . . . the same is in danger to be hewn down and cast into the fire."[40] As history has shown, from the governor down to the common citizen, Missouri was "made to feel the wrath, and indignation, and chastening hand of an Almighty God."[41]

It must have caused the early members of the Church great sorrow when they realized that they would not inherit the bountiful promised

> The time will come when the land of Zion will be redeemed by the Lord.

land the Lord had provided for them. It is evident, however, that the Lord yet desires both the city of Zion and its temple to be redeemed. Although this will not be done until the Lord commands it, when that time comes, the Savior will open the way for the Saints to again inhabit their latter-day *promised land* of Zion.

---

38   AC 342.

39   AC 348.

40   Mormon 8:21.

41   D&C 87:6.

PROSELYTING HELPS

For the gospel to be true, its restoration had to include the assurance of a promised land.

- The scriptures reveal that two great cities will be established in the latter days: Jerusalem and the city of Zion.

- The future existence of Zion was prophesied by the Lord when He visited the Western Hemisphere after His resurrection.

- The tenth article of faith states: "We believe in the literal gathering of Israel and in the restoration of the Ten Tribes; that Zion (the New Jerusalem) will be built upon the American continent; that Christ will reign personally upon the earth; and, that the earth will be renewed and receive its paradisiacal glory."

- On July 20, 1831, the Lord revealed the exact location of Zion: Jackson County, Missouri.

- On August 2, 1831, Sidney Rigdon dedicated Jackson County, Missouri, for the establishment of Zion.

- The city of Zion will have 24 temples to ensure that the Lord's work will go forth.

Severe persecution prevented the Saints from redeeming Zion. However, the restored covenant of Abraham promises the faithful a promised land. Therefore, Zion will yet be redeemed in the Lord's due time. Until then, our task is to share the gospel with our family, our friends, and all of our Father's children, so that they will have the opportunity to participate in that great day.

SECTION III

Restoring the Church of the Firstborn

And he gave some, apostles; and some, prophets; . . . For the perfecting of the saints, for the work of the ministry, for the edifying of the body of Christ.

Ephesians 4:11–12

$\mathcal{P}$rophets

With the deaths of the Lord's Apostles in the meridian of time, prophets ceased functioning upon the earth and did not serve again until the Lord called Joseph Smith as a prophet at the beginning of the Restoration.

There are fifty-three prophets specifically identified either by name or reference in the Old Testament, as well as three prophetesses and a school for prophets.[1] From Paul's writings in the New Testament, we can easily discern that the Lord's Twelve were considered prophets.[2] Paul also identified a man named Agabus as a prophet, although he was not one of the Twelve Apostles.[3] Anna, who recognized Jesus as the long-awaited Messiah when He was brought to the temple as an infant, was identified as a prophetess.[4]

> The Lord's ancient Apostles were considered prophets.

---

1   Prophets 4.
2   Ephesians 2:20; 4:11-12.
3   Acts 11:27-28; 21:10.
4   Luke 2:36.

John the Baptist was asked if he was a reincarnation of the prophet Elias, to which he responded, "No."[5] But the Savior referred to him as the greatest of prophets.[6] Jesus was considered a prophet on several occasions: "And when he was come into Jerusalem, all the city was moved, saying, Who is this? And the multitude said, This is Jesus the prophet of Nazareth of Galilee."[7]

Paul, when writing to the Ephesians, obviously knew of the declaration written hundreds of years before by Amos concerning the need for prophets because he emphasized their importance when he stated that they were necessary to ensure the perfection of the saints, the work of the ministry, and the edification of the body of Christ. He said they would exist forever, or at least until all mankind became unified in the faith and knowledge of the Son of God and became perfect, even as Christ is perfect. He said prophets would be needed until we were no longer like children, tossed to and fro by every wind of doctrine. It was Paul's contention that without prophets and apostles, mankind would be misled by the "slight of men" and that cunning craftiness wherein the wicked lie in wait to deceive.[8]

The Old Testament prophet Amos wrote, "Surely the Lord God will do nothing, but he revealeth his secret unto his servants the prophets."[9] Joseph Smith made two corrections in this verse when he retranslated the Bible. The inspired version reads, "Surely the Lord God will do nothing, *until* he revealeth *the* secret unto his servants the prophets."[10] The conclusion of either version is clear: the Lord will always call and use prophets to do His work. They are integral to His plan of salvation. Without a prophet

> The Lord will always call prophets to do His work.

---

5 John 1:21.

6 Luke 7:26-28.

7 Matthew 14:5; 21:10-11.

8 Ephesians 2:18-22; 4:11-14.

9 Amos 3:7.

10 Inspired Version, Amos 3:7. Italics added to show corrections.

having been called of God in the latter days, the Restoration would never have taken place.

It is interesting that as a practical matter, none of the major Christian religions has ever claimed to be led by a prophet. During the ages that elapsed between the deaths of the Lord's Apostles and the

No religion claimed to have a prophet during the Dark Ages.

restoration of the Gospel in the early 1800s, religionists have claimed to be popes, pastors, priests, reverends, fathers, evangelists, deacons, ministers, etc., but never prophets. They always assumed (and taught) that prophets ended with the Bible.

Why did God stop calling prophets for a season? Perhaps the basic reason is that the people had become so wicked during the Dark Ages that He would not allow them to have prophets. But God will only deal through prophets, so it is only logical to assume that when the time came for Him to restore the true church and gather the righteous for the last time, a prophet would lead the way.

One of the unique evidences of the Restoration was the call of Joseph Smith as the Lord's first prophet of the latter days. There is no doubt that he knew he had received this call since he referred to himself as a prophet, as the following story illustrates.

The call of Joseph Smith as a prophet is one of the unique evidences of the Restoration.

In the latter part of January 1831, Joseph and his wife Emma left New York for Ohio in compliance with the Lord's commandment to initiate the gathering. They arrived there around the first part of February and were welcomed into the house of Newel K. Whitney, one of the brethren who had been converted by Oliver Cowdery and Parley P. Pratt. The Whitney family recorded this event:

> About the first of February, 1831, a sleigh
> containing four persons drove through the

streets of Kirtland and drew up in front of the store of Gilbert and Whitney. One of the men, a young and stalwart personage alighted, and springing up the steps walked into the store and to where the junior partner was standing. 'Newel K. Whitney! Thou art the man!' he exclaimed, extending his hand cordially, as if to an old and familiar acquaintance. 'You have the advantage of me,' replied the merchant, as he mechanically took the proffered hand. 'I could not call you by name as you have me.' '*I am Joseph the Prophet,*' said the stranger smiling. 'You've prayed me here, now what do you want of me?' The Prophet, it is said, while in the East had seen the Whitneys, in vision, praying for his coming to Kirtland.[11]

Further evidence of Joseph's call was provided at the dedication of the Kirtland Temple. During the meeting, Joseph asked the Saints in attendance to "acknowledge the Presidency as Prophets and Seers." They sustained them unanimously by rising. Joseph then presented the Twelve Apostles "as Prophets, Seers, Revelators, and special witnesses." They were also unanimously sustained.[12]

In Nauvoo, Illinois, on January 1, 1843, Joseph was asked if he was a prophet. In response he said, "If any person should ask me if I were a prophet, I should not deny it, as that would give me the lie."[13] On February 8, 1843, he was asked by a brother and sister from Michigan if "a prophet [was] always a prophet." He replied that "a prophet was a prophet only when he was acting as such."[14]

Since the restoration of The Church of Jesus Christ of

11   HC 1:145 ftnt, 146 ftnt. Emphasis added.
12   HC 2:417.
13   HC 5:215.
14   HC 5:265.

Latter-day Saints, the First Presidency and the Twelve Apostles have always been sustained as prophets, seers, and revelators; called of God, as were all the biblical prophets of old. Thus it is that thanks to the prayer of a fourteen-year-old boy, God's prophets are once again upon the earth.

Since the call of Joseph Smith, God's prophets have continuously functioned upon the earth.

PROSELYTING HELPS

Prophets of God are integral to the plan of salvation.

- Both the Old and New Testaments testify that the Lord's gospel will always require prophets.

- From Paul's writings in the New Testament, we know that the Lord's ancient Apostles were considered prophets.

- Joseph Smith's call as a prophet by the Lord is a unique evidence of the Restoration.

- Since Joseph's call, prophets have functioned continuously upon the earth.

The Lord called Joseph Smith as a prophet, just as He did the prophets of old. He has continued to call prophets to lead the Church since that time, and they will continue to do the Lord's work upon the earth until the Second Coming. We can explain to nonmembers that the Lord has again called a living prophet as his spokesman on earth, just as He did with Moses and Isaiah. Inviting our friends to hear the prophet speak in general conference creates an opportunity for them to feel the Spirit and gain a witness of the truth.

And suddenly there came a sound from heaven as of a rushing mighty wind, and it filled all the house where they were sitting.

Acts 2:2

A Rushing Mighty Wind

The Lord tends to use patterns. Since He used a rushing mighty wind and flames of fire to evidence acceptance of His ancient Apostles, it is logical to assume he would use a similar circumstance to evidence the truthfulness of His restored Church and show His approval of the activities of his latter-day church leaders.

There have been occasions when the Lord evidenced His acceptance of certain events in a very unique way. For example, after His resurrection—and for a period of forty days thereafter—the Savior appeared to His Apostles and others on the Eastern Hemisphere to evidence the fact that He had risen from the tomb. Then a most unique miracle occurred involving rushing wind and tongues of fire. The Lord appeared to the Apostles who had assembled just prior to the day of Pentecost (fifty days after the celebration of the Passover) and again commanded them to bear witness of His divinity at Jerusalem, Judaea, Samaria, and "unto the uttermost part of the earth."[1] Thereafter, the Ascension occurred wherein the Savior "was parted" from the Apostles and "carried up into heaven."[2] After the Ascension, the Apostles gathered with some of the disciples to select a replacement for Judas Iscariot, who had betrayed the Savior and then committed suicide. After some deliberation, they selected two: Barsabas and Matthias, both of whom had been with them throughout the Savior's ministry. After they had prayed they cast lots (voted), and Matthias was chosen to replace Judas.[3] "[S]uddenly there came a sound from heaven as of a rushing mighty wind, and it filled all the house where they were sitting."[4] This was immediately followed by the appearance of "cloven tongues like as of fire" that "sat upon each of them."[5] They were immediately filled with the Holy Ghost and spontaneously spoke in tongues, "as the Spirit gave them utterance."[6] This unique event confirmed the Lord's acceptance of the Apostles and acknowledged them as the leaders of His ancient church.

A similar sign of acceptance was given to members of the Lord's restored church on January 17, 1836. The Prophet Joseph Smith and the Twelve were speaking to the Saints gathered in a school house in Kirtland, Ohio. Joseph recorded that the Spirit was so strong that "the gift of tongues came on us . . . like the rushing of a mighty wind."[7] Although this experience compares to that of the early Apostles, an actual duplication of the New Testament phenomena would yet occur.

> The Lord showed approval of his ancient Apostles with a rushing wind and fire.

As the Prophet dedicated the Kirtland Temple on March

---

1   Acts 1:8.
2   Luke 24:51.
3   Acts 1:21–26.
4   Acts 2:2.
5   Acts 2:3.
6   Acts 2:4.
7   HC 2:376.

27, 1836, he sought the Lord's approbation in his prayer when he said, "And
let thy house be filled, as with a rushing mighty wind."[8] The prayer was
accepted by the congregation and the

meeting ended around four in the afternoon. The answer
to Joseph's prayer came later that evening during a meeting
of the priesthood. The following experience is recorded in
the *History of the Church:*

> ... [A] noise was heard like the sound of a
> rushing mighty wind, which filled the Tem-
> ple, and all the congregation simultaneously
> arose, being moved upon by an invisible
> power; many began to speak in tongues and
> prophesy; others saw glorious visions; and
> I beheld the Temple was filled with angels,
> which fact I declared to the congregation.
> The people of the neighborhood came run-
> ning together (hearing an unusual sound
> within ...).[9]

After the rushing wind ceased, those in the neighborhood who had gathered suddenly witnessed the second
evidence of the Lord's acceptance. They saw "a bright light
like a pillar of fire resting upon the Temple."[10]

These manifestations of wind and fire that the Lord
used to witness His approbation of the early Saints' activities specifically compare to the following events recorded
in the Bible and the Book of Mormon:

- An angel of the Lord appeared to Moses in a "flame of
  fire out of the midst of a bush," and God spoke to Mo-

---

8   D&C 109:37.

9   HC 2:428.

10   HC 2:428.

ses and commanded him to bring the children of Israel out of Egypt.[11]

- The Lord used a mighty wind to drive the families of Lehi and Ishmael toward the promised land after their eight-year sojourn in the wilderness subsequent to leaving Jerusalem.[12]

- The Jaredites left the tower of Babel and traveled until they reached the sea shore. Then the Lord directed them to construct eight boats (which were designed without sails and were built to be tight like a dish). When all was prepared, the Lord caused the boats to be driven by a furious wind for three hundred and forty-four days, until the Jaredites reached the promised land the Lord had prepared for them. He also caused sixteen stones to glow with light so that once placed in the boats, the Jaredites would not travel in darkness.[13]

- John the Baptist states that he baptized "with water unto repentance," but that the one who would come after him would baptize "with the Holy Ghost, and with fire."[14]

- When Lehi prayed to the Lord, "there came a pillar of fire and dwelt upon a rock before him; and he saw and heard much."[15]

- A pillar of fire encircled both Nephi 2 and his brother Lehi to protect them from being slain by the armies of the Lamanites.[16]

- Individuals in both the Bible and the Book of Mormon were cast into fiery furnaces and were saved. In the book of Daniel, Shadrach, Meshach, and Abednego were cast into a fiery furnace and received no harm. Those ob-

---

11   Exodus 3:2-4.
12   1 Nephi 18:8.
13   Ether 6:5-8.
14   Matthew 3:11.
15   1 Nephi 1:6.
16   Helaman 5:23-26.

serving looked into the furnace and could see a fourth figure with them, "like unto the Son of God."[17] The Book of Mormon records the story of the Lord's three translated disciples who were cast into a fiery furnace in an attempt to destroy them, but "they came forth receiving no harm."[18]

The singular events involving wind and fire that were witnessed by the members of the Church in Kirtland (and that were subsequently related to others who were not present at those events) confirmed that the Lord had accepted those called as leaders in His restored Church, much like the tongues of flame witnessed His acceptance of His original Apostles during the meridian of time—another unique evidence of the Restoration.

PROSELYTING HELPS

The Lord's use of similar expressions of approbation in the meridian of time and during the Restoration help to support the fact that God is the same yesterday, today, and forever. It gives credence to the restoration of the gospel in the latter days and validates both the Church of Jesus Christ of Latter-day Saints and its leaders.

- A rushing mighty wind and cloven tongues of fire appeared when the Holy Ghost was given to the Lord's ancient Apostles. This occurred on the occasion when Matthias was chosen to replace Judas Iscariot in the Twelve.

- When the Kirtland Temple was dedicated, a rushing

---

17   Daniel 3:20–25.

18   4 Nephi 1:32.

mighty wind filled the temple and after the wind ceased, a bright light like a pillar of fire appeared, resting upon the temple. As in days of old, the Lord was showing His approbation of His restored church and its leaders.

Time after time, using a variety of ways, the Lord has evidenced the fact that the Restoration took place and that the Church of Jesus Christ of Latter-day Saints is true.

The Revelation of Jesus Christ, which God gave unto him, to shew unto his servants things which must shortly come to pass; and he sent and signified it by his angel unto his servant John.

Revelation 1:1

Revelation

Revelation as it was at the time of the Lord's ancient Apostles ceased to exist during the Great Apostasy. Although revelation to the Lord's authorized servants ushered in the latter days, other religionists of Joseph's time believed that there were no such things as visions or revelations, that "all such things had ceased with the Apostles, and there would never be any more of them."[1]

When speaking of the rewards available in heaven, the Apostle Peter confirmed the need for future revelation in our day. He declared, "Blessed be the God and Father of our Lord Jesus Christ, which according to his abundant mercy hath begotten us again unto a lively hope of the resurrection of Jesus Christ from the dead, [t]o an inheritance incorruptible, and undefiled, and that fadeth not away, re-

Revelation was restored in the latter days.

---
1   History of the Church 1:6–7

served in heaven for you, [w]ho are kept by the power of God through faith unto salvation *ready to be revealed in the last time.*"[2] The Lord obviously made known to the prophets of old that revelation—that essential means of communication between God and man—would be restored in the latter days.

When prophesying of the Great Apostasy, Paul declared, "For the time will come when [people] will not endure sound doctrine . . . And | Nephi prophesied that all things would be revealed to the children of men.

they shall turn away their ears from the truth, and shall be turned unto fables."[3] But Nephi, speaking of the Book of Mormon, prophesied that a day would come when "the words of the book which were sealed shall be read upon the house tops; and they shall be read by the power of Christ; and all *things shall be revealed* unto the children of men which ever have been among the children of men, and which ever will be even unto the end of the earth."[4]

Revelation is an interesting concept. When we speak to God, it is | Revelation can come in various forms.

called prayer; when He speaks to us, it is called revelation. Revelation as recorded in the scriptures comes in many forms:

Visions

Visions such as the one John saw on the Isle of Patmos (recorded in the book of Revelation); Elisha's call when he saw a vision of the fiery chariot of Elijah;[5] or the vision Peter, James, and John received on the Mount of Transfiguration.[6]

---

2   1 Peter 1:3-5. Emphasis added.

3   2 Timothy 4:3-4.

4   2 Nephi 27:11. Emphasis added.

5   2 Kings 3:11-12.

6   Matthew 17:1-3.

Dreams

Dreams such as those received by Mary's husband, Joseph, telling him to take her as his wife[7] and instructing him on how to protect the infant Jesus from the edicts of Herod;[8] or the dream Daniel had that revealed Nebuchadnezzar's forgotten dream and its interpretation.[9]

Signs

Signs such as the one given to Hezekiah confirming that he would live another fifteen years,[10] or the sign of the prophet Jonas (when he spent three days in the belly of a great fish) that evidenced the resurrection of Jesus Christ.[11]

Visitations

Visitations such as when Jacob wrestled all night with an angel,[12] or when Jesus appeared to two men after His resurrection as they traveled on the road to Emmaus.[13]

Testimony

Testimonies such as the testimony given to Peter when he responded to the Lord's question, "Whom do men say that I the Son of man am?"[14] or Paul's instructions to the Corinthians wherein he states, "no man can say that Jesus is the Lord, but by the Holy Ghost."[15]

Promise of Reward

Promises such as when Paul declared that the "Spirit

---

7   Matthew 1:20.
8   Matthew 2:13, 20.
9   Daniel 2.
10   Isaiah 38:5-8.
11   Matthew 12:40; Luke 11:29-30.
12   Genesis 32:24-28.
13   Luke 24:13-16.
14   Matthew 16:13-19.
15   1 Corinthians 12:3.

itself beareth witness with our spirit, that we are the children of God: And if children then heirs; heirs of God, and joint-heirs with Christ."[16]

Inspiration

Inspiration such as when Paul declared to Timothy, "All scripture is given by inspiration of God, and is profitable for doctrine, for reproof, for correction, for instruction in righteousness: That the man of God may be perfect, throughly furnished unto all good works";[17] and when Elihu declared to Job, "there is a spirit in man: and the inspiration of the Almighty giveth them understanding."[18]

Feelings and Promptings

Feelings which confirm with our spirit the correctness of our thoughts and actions;

Gifts

Gifts such as those of the Spirit enumerated by Paul in 1 Corinthians: "[T]he manifestation of the Spirit is given to every man . . . for to one is given by the Spirit the word of wisdom; to another the word of knowledge by the same Spirit." Among other gifts that the Lord bestows through the Spirit are faith, healing, prophecy, miracles, discerning of spirits, and tongues. Paul concludes with the admonition to seek the best gifts of faith, hope, and charity (the pure love of Christ).[19]

Denoting Acceptance

Paul declared, "For as many as are led by the Spirit of God, they are the sons of God," and are accepted by Him.[20] Another example of revelation denoting the Lord's

---

16   Romans 8:16-17.

17   2 Timothy 3:16-17.

18   Job 32:8.

19   1 Corinthians 12.

20   Romans 8:14.

acceptance of mankind's activities was seen in the previous chapter where He sent a rushing wind and tongues of flame upon His Apostles in the meridian of time, and again at the dedication of the Kirtland Temple.

Paul provides us with other examples of the use of revelation and the Spirit's role therein. In Romans 8:26–27, he states that the Spirit aids us with our prayers. He "maketh intercession for us with groanings which cannot be uttered . . . he maketh intercession for the saints according to the will of God." Again in Romans 15:18–19, he records that the Spirit will assist in the conversion of the Gentiles.

All of these examples confirm that revelation from the Lord existed in the past. And we know that beginning with Joseph Smith's experience, it exists in the present. However, as noted earlier in the chapter on visions, Joseph met with harsh denunciation when he related his vision of the Father and the Son to a minister of one of the Protestant faiths:

> Revelation existed in the past, just as it does in the present.

> Some few days after I had this vision, I happened to be in company with one of the Methodist preachers, who was very active in the before-mentioned religious excitement, and, conversing with him on the subject of religion, I took occasion to give him an account of the vision which I had had. I was greatly surprised at his behavior; he treated my communication not only lightly, but with great contempt, saying, it was all of the devil, that there were no such things as visions or revelations in these days; that all such things

had ceased with the Apostles, and that there would never be any more of them.[21]

Early in the history of the Church, some brethren questioned Joseph concerning the revelations he had received. Oliver Cowdery raised one of these questions, even claiming that he had discovered an error in verse 37 of what became Section 20 of the Doctrine and Covenants. The exact words of the perceived error read: ". . . and truly manifest by their works that they have received of the Spirit of Christ unto the remission of their sins." Stating that the quotation was erroneous, Oliver *commanded* Joseph "in the name of God to erase those words, that no priestcraft be amongst us!" By such, he was accusing Joseph of priestcraft, and it required considerable effort on Joseph's part to set everyone straight.[22]

> Some questioned the fact that Joseph alone was receiving revelation for the Church.

This problem arose again in Kirtland in early November of 1831 when the revelations Joseph had received were being organized for publication in the Book of Commandments. Joseph had received several revelations between August and November and "some conversation was had [among the brethren] concerning revelation and language."[23] This resulted in a few of the brethren questioning the wording of the revelations and the fact that Joseph alone was receiving them. Because of this, the Lord took a hand in solving the problem by giving Joseph yet another revelation:

> And now I, the Lord, give unto you a testimony of the truth of these commandments which are lying before you.

21 HC 1:6-7.
22 HC 1:105.
23 HC 1:224 .

Your eyes have been upon my servant Joseph Smith, Jun., and his language you have known, and his imperfections you have known; and you have sought in your hearts knowledge that you might express beyond his language; this you also know.

Now, seek ye out of the Book of Commandments, even the least that is among them, and appoint him that is the most wise among you;

Or, if there be any among you that shall make one like unto it, then ye are justified in saying that ye do not know that they are true;

But if ye cannot make one like unto it, ye are under condemnation if ye do not bear record that they are true.[24]

In this revelation, the Lord appears to acknowledge Joseph's limited education (apparently one of the concerns regarding the language of the revelations), but confirmed that the revelations were nonetheless true and written correctly. Then He challenged the wisest among them—or anyone else for that matter—to write a revelation. To simplify the challenge, He stated they could select what they perceived to be the *least* of the revelations and use it as a comparison to the one they authored. If they could write one, fine, their concerns were justified and they did not have to believe in the revelations given to the Prophet. But if they could *not* write one, then their concerns must be set aside and they must testify to the truthfulness of the commandments Joseph had received.

Joseph records that William E. M'Lellin (also spelled McLellin in the *History of the Church*), "as the wisest

> William E. M'Lellin learned that true revelation cannot be faked.

---

24 D&C 67:4-8.

man, in his own estimation, having more learning than sense, endeavored to write a commandment."[25] But he failed, and Joseph noted that it was "an awful responsibility to write in the name of the Lord."

As a result of this experience, a "Testimony of the witnesses to the book of the Lord's commandments" was written to which those who had challenged the accuracy of the revelations were asked to subscribe. This testimony, however, was never incorporated into the Book of Commandments because the press, type, and paper were destroyed by the mob in Missouri before the printing could be completed.[26]

Sometimes we overcomplicate the revelation process (and some eliminate it altogether). However, the simplicity with which Joseph received revelation may best be exemplified by his experience with Sister Vienna Jaques. She was a poor Saint in Kirtland, Ohio, who wanted to join the Saints gathering to Missouri. But she did not possess the means to make the move. Joseph asked the Lord about the problem and the Lord simply directed him to provide Sister Jaques with the funds she needed to go to Zion.[27]

Prior to His betrayal, the Lord promised His Apostles that "the Comforter, which is the Holy Ghost, whom the Father will send in my name, . . . shall teach you all things, and bring all things to your remembrance, whatsoever I have said unto you."[28] We may not be privy to the specific blessings the Lord gave His Apostles, but the promise of the Comforter is available to us all. We must be spiritually attuned and learn how to recognize personal revelation when it comes.

Without revelation, the ability to receive communication from God—

Personal revelation comes through the Holy Ghost.

---

25   HC 1:226.

26   HC 1:224–226.

27   D&C 90:28.

28   John 14:26.

either for an individual's personal enlightenment or for the guidance of the Lord's prophets as they direct the affairs of the Church—the plan of salvation would cease. It is indeed not only one of the most unique evidences of the Restoration, but one of the most important.

PROSELYTING HELPS

Without revelation, mankind could not receive communication from God. However, communication is necessary, not only for personal enlightenment, but for direction of the Lord's church in these the latter days.

- Revelation (communication between God and mankind) as it was at the time of the Lord's ancient Apostles ceased to exist during the Great Apostasy.

- It was prophesied that revelation would be restored in the latter days.

- The prophet Nephi prophesied that all things would be revealed: all things which ever had been among the children of men, and which ever would be, even unto the end of the earth.

- Revelation can be received in many ways: through visions, dreams, signs, visitations, testimony, inspiration, feelings and promptings, gifts, etc.

- Oliver Cowdery and others questioned Joseph Smith's ability to receive and record revelation.

- To prove that Joseph was chosen as His prophet, the Lord challenged others to write a revelation.

- William McLellin, having more learning than sense, attempted to write a revelation and failed.

- Thanks to the Restoration, the Holy Ghost (the Comforter), who facilitates communication (revelation) between God and mankind, is available to us all.

The scriptures reveal that revelation existed in Christ's ancient church, but it was absent during the Great Apostasy. The fact that mankind can again receive revelation in this last dispensation of time is a definitive evidence of the Restoration, and one that is often of great interest to nonmembers. The ability to receive the Lord's help with life's problems—whether personally or through a living prophet—is significant to many people.

*And God hath set some in the
church, first apostles, secondarily
prophets, thirdly teachers . . .*

1 Corinthians 12:28

Apostles

The true church must be founded on an apostolic ministry.

The early church was organized with Apostles who were called and ordained by the Lord, who received a | Christ's ancient church was organized with Apostles.
specific witness of His divinity and His resurrection, and who were given the commission to bear witness of the gospel's truths throughout the world. Therefore, the Lord's true church must be founded on an apostolic ministry that has received a personal witness of the divinity of Jesus Christ and a commission to share this witness with the world.[1]

Christ's Apostles

Christ spent an entire night in seclusion and prayer, counseling with His Father in Heaven, as He prepared to call His Apostles.[2] At dawn, He called to Him those who had been with Him through the early stages of His ministry, and

---

1   1 Corinthians 15:5–8; Ephesians 2:20.
2   Luke 6:12.

from them He chose twelve:[3] Peter, James, John, Andrew, Philip, Bartholomew, Thomas, Matthew, James, Thaddaeus, Simon, and Judas Iscariot. Their subsequent training consumed a major portion of the Lord's ministry.

These men—all Galileans except Judas Iscariot who was a Judean—were not from the privileged classes of Christ's day. They might even be classified as illiterate due to their lack of training in the schools of the time. But they loved the Lord, believed in Him, and stayed with Him throughout the entirety of His mission.[4]

The following facts and traditions are all that is known of the Apostles, but with the exception of Judas Iscariot, it appears they all served the Lord faithfully.

Peter

Peter's given name was Simon,[5] but the Lord changed it to Peter (or "Cephas" in Aramaic).[6] He was married[7] and a fisherman by trade. He and his brother Andrew were

---

3   Luke 6:13.

4   The names of the Twelve Apostles appear in four different places in the New Testament: the three Synoptics and the book of Acts (see Acts 1:13, although the list in Acts excludes Judas Iscariot, who was dead by that time, Matthew 27:5). Because of the different ways the lists are sequenced in the various accounts, it is not possible to determine the seniority of all the Apostles in the quorum. It is interesting to note, however, that the scriptures always list them in groups of four.
    Peter, James, John, and Andrew. In all four New Testament lists, Peter is listed first as the chief Apostle in the Quorum of Twelve. The positions of the other three vary with Andrew, the brother of Peter, occasionally listed second. Although an actual "Quorum of the First Presidency" may not have been established as such, it is evident that Peter was the senior Apostle, with James and John second and third in line.
    Philip, Bartholomew, Thomas, and Matthew. Philip is always listed at the beginning of this group, but after him the order varies in the different renditions. Bartholomew is also known as Nathanael; Matthew's second name is Levi; and Thomas is also known as Didymus, signifying "a twin."
    James, Thaddaeus, Simon, and Judas Iscariot. In this group, James, the son of Alpheus (also known in scriptural history as James II, or James the Less) always heads the list and Judas Iscariot always ends it. Thaddaeus is also known as Lebbaeus or Judas (not Iscariot) and Simon is also known as Zelotes, or the Canaanite.

5   2 Peter 1:1.

6   John 1:42; Matthew 16:18.

7   Matthew 8:14.

business partners with James and John.[8] His early home was in Bethsaida on the west shore of Galilee.[9] Some time later, however, he moved to Capernaum. [10] Although Peter is not credited with writing a gospel, many believe that Mark received his information from him.[11] He (along with James and John) was with the Lord on the Mount of Transfiguration,[12] at the raising of the daughter of Jairus,[13] and in the Garden of Gethsemane.[14]

Peter was usually the first to speak and experiment upon the words of the Lord.[15] He spoke powerfully, both for himself and for the Twelve, when he confessed Jesus as the long-awaited Messiah.[16] He boldly taught the gospel after the Lord's resurrection and was rewarded with imprisonment.[17] From his own writings we learn that he labored in Babylon,[18] which in all likelihood is the name he gave to the city of Rome rather than the actual city on the Euphrates. Peter's greatness is affirmed in the book of Acts. Some of the saints thought so highly of him that they "brought forth the sick into the streets, and laid them on beds and couches, that at the least the shadow of Peter passing by might overshadow some of them."[19] We do not know the exact time or method of Peter's death, but the Lord knew how he would die[20] and Peter foresaw it.[21] It is generally believed that he was crucified upside down in

---

8   Mark 1:16-20; Luke 5:10.

9   John 1:44.

10   Matthew 5:14; Mark 1:21, 30; Luke 4:31, 38.

11   Smith's 504.

12   Matthew 17:1.

13   Mark 5:37.

14   Matthew 26:37.

15   Miracles, Chapter 8.

16   Matthew 16:13-19.

17   Acts 12:1-19.

18   1 Peter 5:13.

19   Acts 5:15.

20   John 21:18-19.

21   2 Peter 1:14.

Rome along with Paul during the persecutions of Emperor Nero circa A.D. 64 and A.D. 68. Finally, as a resurrected being, he (along with James and John) appeared during the Restoration to the Prophet Joseph Smith and restored the Melchizedek Priesthood to the earth.[22]

James and John

These brothers desired to call down fire from heaven upon certain Samaritan villages that had rejected the Lord.[23] Thereafter, the Lord gave them the name "Boanerges," which means "sons of thunder."[24] Through either their own or their mother's petition, they aspired to the highest honors in God's kingdom; namely, to sit by the Lord's side in heaven.[25] James was the first apostolic martyr subsequent to the death of Jesus Christ. He was beheaded by Herod Agrippa I near the time of the Passover, circa A.D. 44.[26] John was apparently a disciple of John the Baptist before he followed the Savior.[27] He obviously had a close relationship with the Lord because he identifies himself as "the disciple whom Jesus loved."[28] The scriptures note that it was John who leaned upon the Lord's bosom at the Last Supper[29] and who stood at the foot of the cross when Jesus was crucified and assumed responsibility for His mother.[30] At the miracle of the second drought of fish, he was the Apostle who initially recognized the resurrected Savior standing on the shore of Galilee.[31] It was there that he received a special blessing from the Lord which allowed him to remain upon

---

22   D&C 27:12.
23   Luke 9:54.
24   Mark 3:17.
25   Mark 10:35-41; Matthew 20:21.
26   Acts 12:1-2.
27   John 1:35-42.
28   John 13:23; 19:26; 20:2.
29   John 13:23, 25.
30   John 19:25-27.
31   John 21:7.

the earth until the Lord's Second Coming.[32] As the years went by, he was eventually banished to the isle of Patmos because of his zeal for teaching the gospel.[33] His gospel emphasized Christ's Judean ministry, whereas the Synoptics (Matthew, Mark, and Luke) focused on the Lord's journeys in Galilee and Perea. John's gospel includes many incidents in the Lord's life that are not mentioned by the other Gospel writers. He was also the author of the book of Revelation and three general epistles to the church.[34]

Andrew

Andrew was Peter's brother and originally a disciple of John the Baptist. Peter initially heard about the Messiah from Andrew[35] and later, Andrew shared in Peter's call to the ministry.[36] However, Andrew is mentioned sparingly throughout the gospels.[37] There are no authentic records of his life or death; however, tradition has it that Andrew was widely traveled and spread the Gospel among the Scythians in what is modern day Russia. Tradition also claims he was put to death upon a cross in Achaia.[38]

Philip

Little is known of Philip other than Jesus found him in Galilee and said to him, "Follow me."[39] He is only mentioned three more times in the Gospels.[40] Tradition has it that he was a chariot driver by profession and died in Hieropolis.

---

32 John 21:21–23; D&C 7.

33 Revelation 1:9.

34 John's epistles are included in the Bible as 1 John, 2 John, and 3 John.

35 John 1:35–42.

36 Matthew 4:18–19.

37 See Mark 13:3–4; John 6:8; 12:20–22.

38 Geikie 46.

39 John 1:43–45.

40 John 6:5–7; 12:20–22; 14:8–9.

Nathanael/Bartholomew.

This is the Apostle in whom Jesus found no guile.[41] The scriptures note that Philip found Nathanael and said to him, "We have found him, of whom Moses in the law, and the prophets, did write, Jesus of Nazareth, the son of Joseph." Nathanael responded, "Can there any good thing come out of Nazareth?"[42] There is not much more known about Nathanael except that he is traditionally thought to have been a shepherd or a gardener.

Thomas/Didymus

We usually remember Thomas as having doubted the resurrection of Christ. However, he was also ready to risk his life for the Lord when Jesus returned to Jerusalem at the request of Lazarus' sisters.[43] Tradition has it that Thomas was killed by being run through with a lance in Persia or India.

Matthew/Levi

Matthew is the author of the first Gospel recorded in the New Testament. At his call, he gave a feast in honor of the Lord—for which Jesus was publicly criticized.[44] Matthew was a publican (tax collector). No mention is made of his ministry and there is no tradition associated with his death.

James (James II)

No particular mention is made of James' ministry. Tradition states that he died by being thrown down from the temple and stoned.

Judas/Lebbaeus/Thaddaeus

Little is known of this Apostle. He asked the Lord a

---

41   John 1:45-51.
42   John 1:45-46.
43   John 11:16.
44   Matthew 9:9-13.

question during the Last Supper: "Lord, how is it that thou wilt manifest thyself unto us, and not unto the world?" In recording this question, John made it clear in his gospel that the speaker was Judas Thaddaeus, and not Judas Iscariot.[45]

Simon Zelotes

Simon was a Canaanite living in Galilee. Prior to his call, he may have been associated with the Zealots who opposed Roman rule.[46] He and Matthew were opposites: Simon hated taxes and Matthew gathered taxes; Simon was extremely patriotic while Matthew was denounced as a servant to an alien ruler. Nothing else is known of him.

Judas Iscariot

Judas served as treasurer for Jesus and the Twelve, but John records that he was dishonest in this trust.[47] On one occasion, he even objected to the waste of valuable oil that Mary used to anoint the Lord's feet.[48] He eventually betrayed the Savior of the World for thirty pieces of silver. The manner of his betrayal indicates that he was covetous, malicious, and vengeful because he personally conducted the band that arrested the Lord in the Garden of Gethsemane that fateful night and singled Him out with an affectionate kiss.[49] John indicates that Satan had entered into Judas.[50] But Judas, "when he saw that he was condemned, repented himself," and returned the thirty pieces of silver to the chief priests and elders saying, "I have sinned in that I have betrayed the innocent blood. ... And he cast down the pieces of silver in the temple, and departed, and went

---

45   John 14:22.
46   Acts 1:13; 5:37; Luke 6:15.
47   John 12:6.
48   John 12:1-7.
49   Matthew 26:49.
50   John 13:2, 27.

and hanged himself." Nonetheless, the Lord classified him as a "son of perdition."[51]

When Matthias was chosen to fill the vacancy in the Twelve created by the death of Judas Iscariot, it became evident that the call of apostle was not to be restricted to the original Twelve.[52] The Apostle Paul, having received a personal witness of Christ's divinity and resurrection, was also called after the Lord's death. As we shall see, this same commission has been given in the latter days to the Apostles of the Restoration, thus maintaining the structure of the original Christ-established gospel.[53]

The Twelve Apostles of the Restoration

Just as the Lord required apostles in the primitive church, so too did He require them in the last days— more incontrovertible evidence of the Restoration.

Apostles are required in the latter days, just as they were in ancient times.

It was June of 1829 when Joseph Smith was first made aware of the fact that he must call apostles. In the revelation recorded as Section 18 of the Doctrine and Covenants, he was told to commission Oliver Cowdery and David Whitmer to select the men who would constitute the first Quorum of the Twelve. Only Oliver Cowdery and David Whitmer of the original three witnesses to the Book of Mormon were mentioned in the revelation. The third witness, Martin Harris, may have been out of favor with the Lord at the time due to his recalcitrance in fulfilling his financial obligations concerning the printing of the Book of Mormon.[54] He eventually paid the printing costs, however, and

---

51 Matthew 27:3-5; Acts 1:18; John 17:12. For a detailed discussion of the Lord's Apostles see Sermons 42-54.

52 Acts 1:23-26.

53 HC 2:193-198.

54 D&C 19.

must have again found favor with the Lord because when the final selection of the Twelve was made on February 14, 1835, Joseph included him.

The Quorum comprised the following: Lyman E. Johnson, Brigham Young, Heber C. Kimball, Orson Hyde, David W. Patten, William E. M'Lellin,[55] John f. Boynton, Orson Pratt, William Smith, Thomas B. Marsh, and Parley P. Pratt.

Of the first Twelve Apostles called during the Restoration, nine were either excommunicated, disfellowshipped, or embittered against Joseph Smith at one time or another prior to the Prophet's death. Only three remained faithful to him, among them the deceased Apostle, David W. Patten. Of the other two Joseph wrote, "Of the Twelve Apostles chosen in Kirtland, and ordained under the hands of Oliver Cowdery, David Whitmer and myself, there have been but two but what have lifted their heel against me—namely Brigham Young and Heber C. Kimball."[56]

This spirit of dissension must have been extremely painful for Joseph, as another of his journal entries implies: "No quorum in the Church was entirely exempt from the influence of those false spirits who are striving against me for the mastery; even some of the Twelve were so far lost to their high and responsible calling, as to begin to take sides, secretly, with the enemy."[57]

In spite of the obvious influence of the adversary, the office of apostle was restored in this dispensation of time and will remain in force, allowing the great men who receive this call to continue to build the Church of Jesus Christ of Latter-day Saints until the Second Coming of the Messiah.

> The office of apostle has been firmly established in the latter days.

---

55 William [Wm] E. M'Lellin's last name is also spelled "McLellin" in other places in church history.

56 HC 5:412.

57 HC 2:488.

PROSELYTING HELPS

Apostles were a key element in the Lord's primitive church. Ephesians 4:11–13 states, "And he gave some, apostles; and some, prophets; and some, evangelists; and some, pastors and teachers; For the perfection of the saints, for the work of the ministry, for the edifying of the body of Christ: Till we all come in the unity of the faith, and of the knowledge of the Son of God, unto a perfect man, unto the measure of the stature of the fulness of Christ." Since apostles are scripturally required, they would be essential in a restored, latter-day church.

- Twelve apostles were called and ordained in Christ's primitive church, and consistently, twelve apostles were called during the restoration of the gospel in the latter days.

- In spite of the efforts of the adversary, the office of apostle was restored in this dispensation of time and remains firmly intact.

The office of apostle as found in the Church of Jesus Christ of Latter-day Saints conforms to the organization Christ had in the primitive church, and is an essential part of the Restoration.

*And when he had called unto him his twelve
disciples [apostles], he gave them power . . .
and commanded them, saying, . . . go, preach,
saying, The kingdom of heaven is at hand.*

Matthew 10:1–7

A Charge to the Twelve

As apostles were called in Christ's primitive
church, and again during the Restoration,
they were given specific instructions.

The authority to again organize the Quorum of Twelve
Apostles was given to Joseph Smith during the Restoration—authority unique to the Church of Jesus Christ of
Latter-day Saints. Once twelve apostles had been called
and ordained they were given specific charges, as were the
Apostles who served with Christ:

To the Lord's Apostles

The Lord's ancient Apostles were to begin actively
proselyting in the towns and villages of Galilee. It was their
first mission without the Savior, and it would be a great
learning experience. To assist them in the work, Jesus gave
them a discourse that covered the following:[1]

---

1   See Matthew 10:1–42; Mark 3:13–19; 6:7–13; and Luke 6:12–16; 9:1–6;
     12:1–12; 22–35 for all ensuing quotes in this section and a complete scrip-
     tural account of the Lord's charge to the Twelve.

Sphere of the work

Although the Twelve would eventually be commanded to go unto all the world,[2] for now the Lord only wanted them to go to the Israelites—the Lord's "lost sheep." He further restricted them to their native province of Galilee. He specifically forbade them to go to the Gentiles and the Samaritans, probably because the Twelve were familiar with the culture and traditions of the Jews and relatively unfamiliar with the mores of the other cultures. The duration of their missions, however, is unknown.

Nature of the work

The Savior specifically instructed the Apostles to only preach repentance and to teach the people that the kingdom of God was at hand. Perhaps He restricted what they could teach because their knowledge at this point was incomplete (although He had given them the priesthood so they could perform miracles and had instructed them to use this gift freely on their missions).

> The Twelve Apostles who served with Christ actively proselyted.

The Lord specifically instructed the Apostles to beware of men. He knew that the ways of the Jewish leadership were such that the Apostles would have nothing to look forward to but persecution. They would be falsely accused, dragged before the Jewish councils and testified against, and scourged in the synagogues. Although the work they were embarking upon and the gospel they would preach would bring peace to the individual, it would also divide brother against brother, father against child, and children against parents. Yet in His instructions, Jesus clearly indicated that they could win over the hearts of men and women through their unselfish devotion and the truthfulness of the gospel.

Personal needs and comforts

The Apostles were to carry neither purse nor script.

---

2   Matthew 28:19.

They were not to indulge in empty courtesies, but were to pay strict attention to their missions by teaching

those who would receive them and casting the dust from their feet on those who would not. He intended them to sacrifice all their personal desires to follow Him, even though He offered no earthly reward. Their basic equipment was simple: they were to go in essentially the clothing they had on their backs and they were not to take extra coats, shoes, or staves to assist them in their travels. "Are not five sparrows sold for two farthings, and not one of them is forgotten before God?" He asked, obviously implying that the Apostles were much more important than sparrows. He also comforted them by explaining that in the end, nothing would be lost. Even the hairs on their heads were numbered to the Father.

It is evident that the Lord intended His Apostles to eventually abandon their vocations and even forsake family ties, if necessary, so that the work of the gospel could go forth. Through His instructions, they would learn to curb their reactions to persecution and suppress even justified resentment in order to completely mold their lives to His service. They could look for a reward in heaven, but they would not find one on the earth; in this world they would be "hated of all men, for [His] name's sake."[3] But the Lord assured them that His eye would be continually upon them. As bleak as their prospects were, the Apostles knew that their salvation lay in the Lord's hands and they only need fear he who could destroy their souls—the adversary.

Results

It would appear that Jesus chose to send the Twelve on missions at this particular time because of the great success He had already enjoyed in His own ministry. They must have gone forth with enthusiasm for they returned with

---

3   Mark 13:13.

joy, noting that many multitudes had followed them. Their success was obviously considerable, but it may have been related more to their miracles than to their message. The Savior returned to Capernaum to receive the Twelve from their missions at about the same time that the news reached Him of the death of John the Baptist. Perhaps John's death is the reason the Lord cautioned the Apostles at that time not to be overly elated with their success. Still, their missions must have brought the Savior great joy.

Although the Twelve were young in their callings and would continue to follow and learn from Jesus throughout His ministry, it was time for them to "take up their cross." They had to be willing to do whatever was necessary to promulgate the gospel and build the kingdom of God upon the earth. Whether they completely understood what *taking up their cross* meant is not clear, but the analogy would have impressed and possibly terrified them because crucifixion—being hung on a cross to die—was a method of capital punishment used by the Romans of their day.

To the Apostles of the Restoration

Of the twelve Apostles called during the Restoration, only ten were ordained and blessed at the time of their calling. These ordinations occurred on February 14 and 15 of 1835. Elders Thomas B. Marsh and Orson Pratt were absent at the time serving missions, and were ordained later.

After the ten were ordained, Oliver Cowdery gave them a charge. His first comments went directly to Parley P. Pratt. Among other things, Parley was required to bear the same testimony that the Lord's original Apostles had borne; i.e., "that they had seen the Savior after He rose from the dead." Then Oliver gave a general charge to the Twelve that consisted of at least seven specific parts:[4]

---

4   See HC 2:180–200 & ftnts for all ensuing quotes in this section and for the
      complete instructions to the Twelve in the latter days.

1. They were to preach the Gospel to every nation. If they failed to do this, they would fall short of their duty and "great [would] be [their]

   The Twelve Apostles of the Restoration were instructed to preach the gospel to every nation.

   condemnation; for the greater the calling the greater the transgression."

2. They were to cultivate "great humility." Oliver warned them about the flattery of men and against being captivated "by worldly objects," because he knew "the pride of the human heart."

3. They were to place their ministry first since the souls of men were committed to their charge.

4. Up to that moment, they had been indebted to other men for their testimonies. Now they were required to receive a testimony from heaven for themselves so that they could bear witness of two things: (a) that they knew of the truthfulness of the Book of Mormon, and (b) that they had "seen the face of God." He informed them that this testimony was more than the testimony received from an angel and was necessary because they would have to bear this testimony to the world. Then he gave them this exhortation: "Never cease striving until you have seen God face to face."

5. Although the Twelve had been ordained, Oliver said their ordination would not be full and complete "till God has laid His hand upon you." Just as the Savior laid His hands upon the first Twelve, so would He lay His hands upon the Apostles of the latter days.

6. The adversary would seek their lives. Why? Because "the adversary has always sought the lives of the servants of God." Then Brother Cowdery counseled them that they should be fully prepared "at all times" to sacrifice their lives for the work, "should God require them."

7. Oliver said the Lord's Apostles hold the "keys" of the

ministry; consequently, they are required to take the gospel to all nations and to gather Israel. Yes, they would be rejected, but also accepted; it was their responsibility to warn the world. "If you will not warn them," Brother Cowdery admonished, "others will, and you will lose your crowns."

After completing this charge to the Twelve (which Parley P. Pratt referred to as Oliver's "Oath and Covenant of the Apostleship"), Oliver took each of the brethren by the hand and said, "Do you with full purpose of heart take part in this ministry, to proclaim the Gospel with all diligence, with these your brethren, according to the tenor and intent of the charge you have received?" Each of them answered in the affirmative.

With the completion of these instructions, the work of the kingdom in the latter days commenced, mirroring the work that the Lord had initiated in the meridian of time.

PROSELYTING HELPS

The Lord instructed Joseph Smith to call twelve apostles during the Restoration, mirroring His call of the Twelve Apostles who assisted Him during His earthly ministry. Both sets of Apostles were given instructions to guide them in their missions, instructions that also apply to all subsequent Apostles called to do the Lord's work.

• The Twelve Apostles who served with Christ were told to actively proselyte in the towns and villages of Galilee. Later, they would be instructed to take the gospel to all the world.

• The Lord instructed His Twelve to only preach repentance and warn the people that the kingdom of God was at hand.

- These Apostles did not carry purse or script. They were expected to sacrifice their personal desires if they wanted to follow Christ and do His work.

- The Apostles of the Restoration were instructed to preach the gospel to every nation. They, too, were to place the ministry first in their lives. They were also instructed to bear witness to the existence of God and to obtain a sure testimony of the truthfulness of the Book of Mormon.

Today, just as in Christ's primitive church, the Twelve Apostles of the Church of Jesus Christ of Latter-day Saints bear the special charge of witnessing the divinity of the Savior to the world. But the Twelve Apostles alone cannot meet the demands of this great work. As the Savior's Second Coming approaches, it becomes increasingly important that whenever possible, all active members of the Church should provide the opportunity for their family members, friends, and other associates to hear the gospel.

*Behold, I will send my messenger, and he shall
prepare the way before me: and the Lord, whom
ye seek, shall suddenly come to his temple . . .*

Malachi 3:1

Temples

The Lord has historically required His people
to construct temples where they could worship. Temples give the Lord a home on earth
where He can communicate with His prophets. Temple construction in the latter days
continues the precedent God established in
the scriptures.

When Adam came out of the Garden of Eden, he built an
altar and offered sacrifices to the Lord. He had been commanded to make these offerings, but he did not know why
until an angel visited him and told him that the sacrifices
were made in "similitude of the sacrifice of the Only Begotten of the Father," an event that would occur sometime in
the future.[1] Therefore, from that time until the children of
Israel were led out of captivity in Egypt, altars were considered places of worship.

From the time of the Exodus and up through the restoration of the gospel in the latter days, altars have been

---

1   Moses 5:5-7.

housed in three types of temples: sacrificial, restoration, and endowment. | There are three types of temples.

Sacrificial Temples

The first sacrificial temple was constructed by King Solomon circa 953 B.C.[2] Prior to that time, the Israelites' sacrificial worship was performed in a traveling tabernacle. The Lord commanded Moses to build this tabernacle shortly after he led the children of Israel out of Egypt, describing in detail the pattern of its construction, its contents, and its implements of worship. When it was completed, He commanded the males of the tribe of Levi to officiate therein as priests.[3]

The Israelites carried the tabernacle with them as they wandered in the wilderness—erecting it when they stopped and packing it up when they moved on. Once they entered the promised land, the tabernacle continued to be transported from area to area so that the various tribes could worship correctly under the Law of Moses. However, with the construction of Solomon's temple, use of the tabernacle ceased and sacrificial worship was confined to the temple in Jerusalem.

Solomon's temple stood for approximately four hundred years, up until Nebuchadnezzar conquered Jerusalem and looted and destroyed it | A sacrificial temple will yet be constructed on the temple mount in Jerusalem.

circa 570 B.C. It remained in its ruined condition until it was reconstructed through the efforts of Nehemiah and Ezra, circa 500 B.C.—approximately seventy years after its destruction. It was plundered and damaged again by the Seleucid Kings circa 168 B.C. and was rededicated circa 165 B.C. by the Maccabees. From then until its final destruction

---

2   1 Kings 6:1.

3   Exodus 25–27.

by the Romans in A.D. 70, the Jews celebrated its restoration with what they called the Feast of Dedication.[4]

The Jews continued to worship in Solomon's temple until Herod the Great began his expansion and new construction around 19 B.C. (It is Herod the Great's temple in Jerusalem that is referred to in the New Testament.)

| Solomon and Herod built sacrificial temples on the temple mount in Jerusalem.

Up until the temple was finally destroyed by the Romans, circa A.D. 70, it was used to perform the sacrifices required under the Law of Moses. A sacrifice was performed morning and evening to open and close each day. Various other sacrifices were performed at holidays and for individual needs as required (or available) under the Law.[5] Jesus and His Apostles also taught in the temple,[6] and on two occasions the Lord cleansed the temple of those who were using it improperly.[7]

Today, the wailing wall in Jerusalem (part of the retaining wall built by Herod the Great so he could expand the size of the mount that held the temple) is the only remaining structure of Herod's original temple. In its heyday, however, it was a magnificent structure that inspired the comment, "He that has not seen the Temple of Herod, has never known what beauty is."[8]

It is prophesied that the temple will be reconstructed in Jerusalem a third time upon the same temple mount as the temples of antiquity. Many prophets have seen this temple in vision. Ezekiel described its size and layout.[9] Isaiah described its beauty stating, "The glory of Lebanon shall come unto thee, the fir tree, the pine tree, and the box together, to beautify the place of my sanctuary; and I

---

4   John 10:22.

5   Acts 21:26.

6   Matthew 21:23; Acts 5:42.

7   John 2:12-25; Mark 11:15-19. See also Sermons 67-72.

8   Ed 1:120.

9   Ezekiel 40.

will make the place of my feet glorious."[10] Zechariah was also told that the Lord's house would again be built in Jerusalem,[11] and he saw in vision the day when "the foundation of the house of the Lord of Hosts was laid."[12] He also saw those who would build and occupy it.[13] Finally, the Lord showed this magnificent temple to the prophet Wilford Woodruff, again confirming that it would be built in Jerusalem in the latter days.[14]

According to the Doctrine and Covenants, once the temple in Jerusalem is built, sacrifice will again be offered by the sons of Levi "unto the Lord in righteousness."[15] No ordinances with which we are familiar today were ever performed in this temple.

Restoration Temple

The Kirtland Temple was a temple of restoration. The Lord commanded the Saints to build it in a revelation given December 27, 1832 (Section 88 of the Doctrine and Covenants). There the Lord instructed the people to build a "house of prayer, a house of fasting, a house of faith, a house of learning, a house of glory, a house of order, a house of God." On June 1, 1833, Joseph recorded that preparations were underway to "commence a house of the Lord," in spite of the poverty of the membership.[16] He noted that even the size of the building, "fifty-five feet wide, and sixty-five feet long, in the inner court," was received by revelation.[17]

A newly-formed building committee sent a subscription circular

The Kirtland Temple is the only temple of restoration.

---

10   Isaiah 60:13.

11   Zechariah 1:16.

12   Zechariah 8:9.

13   Zechariah 6:13-15; 8:7, 9.

14   JD 18:111.

15   D&C 13:1.

16   HC 1:349.

17   HC 1:352.

throughout the branches of the Church calling for the members to support the construction of the temple with their donations—the main source of construction funds. The circular explained that the temple was being constructed as a House of the Lord and a place where the School of the Prophets could meet.[18] Joseph noted in his journal that on Thursday, June 25, 1835, there was a meeting in Kirtland where $6,232.50 was subscribed. Included in the subscriptions were the following: Joseph Smith, $500.00; Oliver Cowdery, $750.00; W.W. Phelps, $500.00; John Whitmer, $500.00; and Frederick G. Williams, $500.00. Joseph's journal then states that all of the subscriptions were "paid within one hour, and the people were astonished."[19]

On June 5, 1833, the first load of stone for the temple arrived from the quarry and the trench for the walls commenced. On July 23, 1833, the cornerstones were laid "after the order of the Holy Priesthood."[20] But all did not run smoothly. There was a considerable amount of opposition from the native inhabitants of the area during the time the temple was under construction. Heber C. Kimball recorded the following in his journal:

> The Church was in a state of poverty and distress, in consequence of which it appeared almost impossible that the commandments could be fulfilled [relative to the Kirtland Temple]; at the same time our enemies were raging and threatening destruction upon us, and we had to guard ourselves night after night, and for weeks were not permitted to take off our clothes, and were obliged to lay with our fire locks in our arms.[21]

---

18 HC 1:349–350.

19 HC 2:234.

20 HC 1:400.

21 *Times and Seasons*, 6: 771.

In spite of this adversity, the building was dedicated on March 27, 1836.[22] In this antagonistic climate, however, once the Church left Kirtland and the temple was abandoned, it was eventually taken over by apostates and the mob.[23]

The temple was constructed with pulpits at both its west and east ends. The congregation sat in the middle. The pews could be reversed to observe either pulpit area. The pulpit on the west was for the Melchizedek Priesthood functionaries and the eastern pulpit was designated for leaders of the Aaronic Priesthood. Choir seats were located in the four corners of the room. There were curtains that traversed the room—both north to south and east to west—that could be dropped or raised at any time, thereby partitioning the room into four different areas, if desired.[24]

Nine rules governed visitors to the temple:

1. No one could interrupt the speaker by "whispering, laughing, talking, menacing gestures, leaving in a disorderly manner, or by indignities." Should anyone do so, they would be punished by whatever lawful means were available, and by ejection from the house.

2. Insults to officiating officers were considered insults to the entire body of the Church.

3. Persons were not permitted to go up the stairs (from the first floor) during meetings.

4. No one could explore the house without an appointed escort.

5. No one could go into the pulpits other than those appointed to use the same.

6. It was prohibited to cut, mark, or mar the inside or outside

---

22 The dedicatory prayer for the Kirtland Temple is recorded in Section 109 of the Doctrine and Covenants. The pulpits were dedicated and consecrated to the Lord prior to the dedication of the temple proper.

23 HC 7:484.

24 HC 2:399 ftnt, 411.

of the temple with a knife, pencil, or other instrument. Violators would be punished as the law permitted.

7. Children could not assemble to play on the temple grounds. Parents would be responsible for any damage they caused.

8. All persons, both believers or unbelievers, were to be treated with respect.

9. No member could be denied access to the house.

By 7:00 a.m. on the day scheduled for the dedication, approximately five or six hundred Saints were lined up waiting for the doors to open. The doors opened at 8:00 a.m. and between nine hundred and one thousand persons were seated. Joseph, Sidney, and Oliver acted as ushers. The meeting proper began at 9:00 a.m. As the meeting commenced, additional ushers were posted at the doors to receive donations to help pay for the temple's outstanding construction costs. Nine hundred sixty-three dollars were received.

After the opening song and prayer, Sidney Rigdon spoke for two and a half hours "in his usual logical manner."[25] There was additional singing followed by a short address from the Prophet. Then the quorums and the congregation were called upon to sustain the Presidency of the Church as prophets and seers, and to acknowledge the Twelve Apostles as prophets, seers, revelators, and special witnesses to all nations of the earth. The congregation acknowledged its approbation of these proceedings by rising, and for the first time since the advent of the Dark Ages, a prophet of God and twelve apostles were officially functioning upon the earth.[26] The Seventies were sustained next, then the bishops, their counselors, and the various priesthood leaders officiating in both Kirtland and

---

25   HC 2:414.

26   HC 2:417.

Zion. All sustaining was done by the congregation rising and was unanimous in every instance.[27] Another hymn was sung and then the dedicatory prayer was offered by the Prophet Joseph Smith, who noted that the prayer had been received by revelation.[28] Again a hymn was sung and then the congregation was asked to accept the dedicatory prayer and acknowledge that the house had been dedicated, which they did. The sacrament was then administered to all present.

Many of the brethren testified that they saw angels in attendance at the dedication. It was even claimed that one came in through a window and sat between Frederick G. Williams and "Father Smith" (Joseph's father). After the sacrament, several brethren gave short talks. Then Sidney Rigdon again spoke and prayed, after which the entire congregation shouted, "hosanna, hosanna, hosanna to God and the Lamb," three times, sealing it each time with, "amen, amen, and amen." Next, Brigham Young spoke in tongues and David W. Patten interpreted. Brother Patten also spoke in tongues. Joseph then blessed the congregation and the meeting adjourned at "a little past four o'clock p.m." The meeting had lasted seven hours.[29]

In the evening, the quorums of the priesthood reassembled in the temple and Joseph instructed them concerning the spirit of prophecy and the ordinance of the washing of feet. He encouraged those present to participate in this ordinance. Thus was restored the ordinance that the Savior had instituted with His Apostles at the end of His ministry.[30] The purpose of the ordinance lies in John 13:13–16:

> Ye call me Master and Lord: and ye say well;
> for so I am.
>   If I then, your Lord and Master, have

---

27   HC 2:418.
28   HC 2:420 et seq.; D&C 109.
29   HC 2:427–428.
30   John 13:4–14.

washed your feet; ye also ought to wash one another's feet.

For I have given you an example, that ye should do as I have done to you.

Verily, verily, I say unto you, The servant is not greater than his lord; neither he that is sent greater than he that sent him.

After the brethren finished performing this ordinance, George A. Smith rose and began to prophesy. Suddenly "a noise was heard like the sound of a rushing mighty wind, which filled the Temple." This was followed by many spiritual manifestations:

All the congregation simultaneously arose, being moved upon by an invisible power; many began to speak in tongues and prophesy; others saw glorious visions; and I beheld the Temple was filled with angels, which fact I declared to the congregation. The people of the neighborhood came running together (hearing an unusual sound within, and seeing a bright light like a pillar of fire resting upon the Temple), and were astonished at what was taking place. This continued until the meeting closed at eleven p.m.[31]

There were four hundred and sixteen "official members" present at this evening meeting who witnessed or experienced these manifestations.[32]

On Tuesday, March 29, 1833, Joseph Smith, Frederick G. Williams, Sidney Rigdon, Hyrum Smith, and Oliver Cowdery conducted another meeting in the temple where

31   HC 2:428.
32   HC 2:428.

many ordinances were performed. The priesthood brethren worshiped in the temple all night and at 8:00 a.m., Joseph stated that he had now completed the organization of the Church.[33] He then left the meeting and the Twelve officiated throughout the day and night, adjourning at five o'clock the next morning. It was recorded that during that time, "[t]he Savior made His appearance to some, while angels ministered to others . . . it was an endowment indeed."[34]

On Sunday, April 3, 1836, a remarkable event took place in the Kirtland Temple. After the sacrament had been passed, the curtain of the temple was drawn, with Joseph and Oliver remaining behind the curtain in front of the west pulpit. They both knelt and prayed silently. As their prayer ended, a vision unfolded before their eyes. They saw the Lord standing on the "breastwork of the pulpit," but like prophets of old, they had difficulty describing His countenance. Joseph wrote that the Lord's "eyes were as a flame of fire; the hair of his head was white like the pure snow; his countenance shone above the brightness of the sun; and his voice was as the sound of the rushing of great waters."[35] The Lord declared that their sins were forgiven them and that He accepted the temple that had been built to His name. Immediately upon this vision closing another vision opened and Joseph and Oliver saw Moses, who had come to restore the keys for the gathering of Israel. Then Elias appeared and restored the Gospel [or covenant] of Abraham. Finally, Elijah the prophet came forth and restored the sealing power of the priesthood in fulfillment of the prophecy found in Malachi, which states, "Behold, I will send you Elijah the prophet before the coming of the great and dreadful day of the Lord: And he shall

> Priesthood keys were restored in the Kirtland Temple.

---

33   HC 2:432.

34   HC 2:432–433.

35   D&C 110:3.

turn the heart of the fathers to the children, and the heart of the children to their fathers, lest I come and smite the earth with a curse."[36]

After all of these miraculous events surrounding the dedication of the Kirtland Temple concluded, the temple was generally used as a simple meeting house. The School of the Prophets was housed on the second floor and administrative offices filled the space on the higher floors, including an office in which Joseph pursued the work of translation. These functions continued until the Church left Kirtland. There is no record of endowments as we now know them ever having been performed in the Kirtland Temple. Once the keys necessary for the restoration of the gospel had been restored, the purpose of that temple had been fulfilled.

Endowment Temples

The Nauvoo Temple, as with all temples that have been constructed since the Kirtland era, was an endowment temple, and all of the ordinances that are known to be performed in temples today were performed there.

Joseph received the revelation to erect the Nauvoo Temple on January 19, 1841,[37] and shortly thereafter, he employed William Weeks as the architect.

> All temples constructed after the Kirtland Temple are endowment temples.

He and Brother Weeks disagreed on the design of the windows at one point (Joseph wanted round windows inserted between the floors for light and Brother Weeks felt they should be semicircular). Joseph told him that he "would have the circles, if he had to make the Temple ten feet higher than it was originally calculated." Joseph had seen in vision the "splendid appearance of [the] building

---

36   Malachi 4:5-6.

37   D&C 124:27.

illuminated," and insisted that it be constructed according to the pattern he had been shown.[38]

Baptism for the dead as practiced in New Testament times[39] was the first temple ordinance to be restored during the Restoration. Initially, the Saints performed this ordinance in the Mississippi River, but with the construction of the Nauvoo Temple, a baptismal font was "upon the earth." The Lord stated its purpose: ". . . that they, my saints, may be baptized for those who are dead—For this ordinance belongeth to my house. . . ."[40] On October 2, 1841, the Prophet made the following declaration in General Conference: "There shall be no more baptisms for the dead, until the ordinance can be attended to in the Lord's House; and the Church shall not hold another General Conference, until they can meet in said house. *For thus saith the Lord!*" Consequently, until their expulsion from Illinois, the Saints struggled to build and complete the Nauvoo Temple.

Raising funds for the temple was a slow process, but the work went forth. In addition to donations of money, the brethren were asked to give one-tenth of their time to assist in the building's construction—which they willingly did. Sadly, however, after the martyrdom of Joseph and Hyrum Smith in Carthage Jail, the construction of the temple could not be completed before the Saints were forced to leave Illinois. The last capstone[41] was placed on December 6, 1844, and several rooms of the temple were dedicated as they were completed. Endowments and other ordinances commenced in the temple on December 10, 1845.[42]

---

38   HC 6:196–197.

39   1 Corinthians 15:29.

40   D&C 124:29–30.

41   A capstone is a finishing or protective stone that forms the top of an exterior masonry wall or building. For a detailed description of the capstones on the Nauvoo Temple, see HC 7:323.

42   HC 7:541. The endowment was first given on May 4, 1842, on the second floor of Joseph's red brick store (HC 5:2), and continued on a limited basis until they began sessions in the dedicated areas of the Nauvoo Temple in 1845. On February 8, 1846, the building was dedicated to the "Most High" by the Quorum of the Twelve. No further endowments were given after that

Three nonmember groups were allowed to enter the edifice *after* areas had been dedicated. On December 27, 1845, United States Deputy Marshal Roberts was admitted as he searched for the Twelve Apostles and other Church leaders. He inspected most of the temple and when he entered the attic hall, he was asked to remove his boots and hat. He complied, but he found nothing. He returned around two o'clock that same afternoon and searched again for about one-half hour. (A humorous incident had taken place prior to this search. Several federal officers and some U.S. troops had come to Nauvoo with the intent of arresting Brigham Young and Amasa Lyman. They eventually came to the front doors of the temple intending to search it. Brigham's coach was brought to the front door and William Miller put on Brigham's cap and Brother Kimball's cloak and attempted to get into the carriage. The marshal arrested him on a writ "from the United States court, charging him with counterfeiting the coin of the United States." After some jovial interrogation which finally revealed who had been arrested, Brother Miller was released. The incident became known as the "Bogus Brigham" incident.)[43]

The second nonmember group to enter the temple after its dedication comprised two Catholics, Messrs. Tucker and Hamilton. The Church attempted to sell its property prior to leaving Nauvoo and one of the organizations interested in the temple was the Catholic Church. The above two gentlemen visited Nauvoo and examined the temple. Brigham offered to lease the building to them for thirty-five years. The only cost for the lease was the stipulation that the lessee finish the building's construction. Nothing came of the offer, however.[44]

The third nonmember visit was made by General John J. Hardin and his troops more than a year after the death of

---

date as the Saints were about to leave Nauvoo for the West (HC 7:580).

43   HC 7:549-551.

44   HC 7:539-541.

the Prophet. It occurred on September 30, 1845. The General had brought his troops into Nauvoo on the pretense of searching for two dead bodies of "unknown" men. They searched the temple, the Masonic Hall, the Nauvoo House, and the stables at the Mansion House. In the stables they ran their swords into a pile of manure, as "if they expected to prick some dead bodies and make them squeal." After a fruitless search, they cross-examined Caleb Baldwin. "Most of the questions asked were designed to find out where the bodies of Joseph and Hyrum Smith were buried."[45]

One of the more unusual activities that occurred in the temple was dancing. The first dance took place on December 30, 1845, at around eleven-thirty in the evening—after the endowment sessions had been completed for the day. It began with a few members dancing to the accompaniment of Brother Hanson's violin along with Brother Elisha Averett on the flute. Brigham Young reported that the "spirit of dancing increased until the whole floor was covered with dancers." He noted that, "while we danced before the Lord, we shook the dust from off our feet as a testimony against this nation."[46] This merriment was short lived, however. On January 6, 1846, Brigham requested that all "dancing and merriment should cease, lest the brethren and sisters be carried away by vanity."[47]

Another interesting event occurred on February 9, 1846, when the roof was discovered on fire at 3:30 in the afternoon. An alarm was sounded and Willard Richards called for the brethren to bring buckets. The buckets were filled with water and lines formed to pass them in "quick succession." The fire lasted for about one-half hour. It was caused "by the stovepipe being overheated [while] drying the [temple] clothing in the upper room."[48]

---

45 HC 7:447-448.
46 HC 7:557.
47 HC 7:566.
48 HC 7:581.

Once the Nauvoo Temple opened for endowments, the Saints literally flocked to the city to receive them. On January 12, 1846, Brigham recorded the following: "[Such is the] anxiety manifested by the saints to receive the ordinances [of the Temple], and . . . [such is the] anxiety on our part to administer to them, that I have given myself up entirely to the work of the Lord in the Temple night and day, not taking more than four hours sleep, upon an average, per day, and going home but once a week."[49] On January 20, he reported that public prejudice was so strong against the Church that the brethren "determined to continue the administration of the ordinances of endowment night and day."[50] Even after Brigham announced that they would not perform any more endowments, on February 3, 1846, "the House of the Lord was thronged all day." On that occasion, he reported that he walked "some distance from the Temple supposing the crowd would disperse," but on returning, he found the house "filled to overflowing." Looking upon the multitude with compassion and sensing their anxiety, Brigham wrote, "[A]s they were thirsting and hungering for the word, we continued at work diligently in the House of the Lord."[51] Finally, Brigham and the Twelve had to leave Nauvoo and thereafter, prayer meetings were held in the temple each night "for the preservation of the Saints" until the exodus was complete.

When Brigham left Nauvoo for the last time, he recommended that the keys to the temple be left in the care of one Judge Owens, and the building itself consigned to the hands of the Lord. But on November 19, 1848, the structure was set on fire by a man named Joseph Agnew. The conflagration was not discovered until around three o'clock in the morning and the building was so engulfed at that point that no attempt was made to save it. The fire was

---

49   HC 7:567.

50   HC 7:570.

51   HC 7:579.

reported the next day in the *Nauvoo Patriot*. In describing the temple and the person who put it to flame, the article stated, "To destroy a work of art, at once the most elegant and the most renowned in its celebrity of any in the whole west, would, we should think, require a mind of more than ordinary depravity."[52] Then in 1850, a tornado toppled one of the temple's walls and two other walls were pulled down soon thereafter for fear that they might fall of their own accord and injure someone. The last wall was razed in 1865. Many of the stones from the temple were taken by local citizens and used in private construction, and can still be seen throughout the city today.

What was left of the temple site in 1849 was purchased by the Icarians, a group that followed the teachings and ideals of French philosopher Etienne Cabet. They had left France and settled in Texas because of persecution. When they heard that the Mormons had left Nauvoo, they moved there in 1849 in hopes of acquiring land and developing their own utopian society. They purchased the temple lot for $2,000 from people who had claimed the property after the exodus of the Saints, but dissension arose between factions of the group and they divided. Cabet and other of his followers moved to St. Louis, Missouri; the rest remained in Nauvoo. A member of the Nauvoo group named Emile Baxter eventually developed a winery, and the temple lot property was turned into a vineyard.

Over the years, various portions of the original temple site were purchased and donated to the LDS Church. The Church finally completed the acquisition of the entire property in 1966. For the next thirty-three years, the property remained vacant with only a small monument—including one of the original "sun stones"—marking the site of the original edifice.

During the final session of the April 1999 General Conference, President Gordon B. Hinckley announced that the

---

52   HC 7:617-618 ftnts.

Church would rebuild the Nauvoo Temple. They broke ground on October 24, 1999. The intent was to construct the exterior of the new temple as closely as possible to the appearance of the old edifice. Several prints from early photographs of the temple were available, as well as two of William Weeks' architectural drawings of the facade; therefore, it was possible to reconstruct the new temple quite accurately. By June 2002, the new Nauvoo Temple was finished. It was dedicated on June 27, 2002.

PROSELYTING HELPS

Temples are the hallmark of the Lord's people. They have had varying functions, but are the same in that they all contain altars where the Lord's work can take place.

Through the centuries, three types of temples have been constructed: sacrificial, restoration, and endowment.

Sacrificial
- The Israelites initially conducted the sacrifices required under the Law of Moses in a portable tabernacle. Once they had inherited their promised land, King Solomon constructed a permanent temple in Jerusalem. It stood for approximately four hundred years before it was destroyed by King Nebuchadnezzar circa 570 B.C.

- Herod the Great reconstructed and expanded the temple circa 19 B.C. It was again used to perform sacrifices under the Law of Moses until it was finally destroyed by the Romans circa A.D. 70.

Restoration
- The Kirtland Temple was the only restoration temple built. It was dedicated by the Prophet Joseph Smith

on March 27, 1836. The keys to the gathering of Israel, the covenant of Abraham, and the sealing power of the priesthood of God were all restored in the Kirtland Temple in April of 1836.

- Once the keys necessary for the restoration of the gospel had been restored, the Kirtland Temple was generally used as a meeting house. The upper floors were used for the School of the Prophets and for administrative offices.

Endowment
- Starting with the Nauvoo Temple, all modern temples are endowment temples.

- The ordinances of baptism, the endowment, and sealings (including marriage for time and eternity) are performed in endowment temples.

- After the Saints left Nauvoo, the Nauvoo Temple was burned by an arsonist. Many of the stone walls were later destroyed in a tornado, and the remaining walls were pulled down soon thereafter so they would not fall and injure someone.

- Construction started in 1999 on a replica of the Nauvoo Temple. It was built on the original temple site and was dedicated in 2002 by President Gordon B. Hinckley.

- Today, there are well over one hundred endowment temples worldwide.

Modern temples continue to carry on the Lord's work of salvation, both for the living and for the dead. A spirit of peace and meditation is available to those who serve and/or attend the temples. It is well worth the effort for individuals to put their lives in order so that they may go and enjoy the spirit of the Lord's house.

Behold, I will send you Elijah the prophet
before the coming of the great and dread-
ful day of the Lord; and he shall turn the
heart of the fathers to the children, and the
heart of the children to their fathers, lest
I come and smite the earth with a curse.

Malachi 4:5–6

The Sealing Power

In the book of Matthew, the Lord gave His Apostles the keys of the kingdom of heaven and told them that whatever they sealed (or loosened) on earth would be sealed (or loosened) in heaven. This same sealing power was restored in the Kirtland Temple during the Restoration and is a unique component of the Church of Jesus Christ of Latter-day Saints.

On April 3, 1836, the prophet Elijah appeared to Joseph Smith and Oliver Cowdery in the Kirtland Temple and restored the keys to the sealing power of the priesthood, thus fulfilling the above prophecy in Malachi.[1] The restoration of these keys made it possible for temple work to be performed in the latter days for both the living and the dead.

The book of Matthew indicates that the Lord had prom-

---

1   Malachi 4:5-6.

ised this same sealing power to His Apostles: "And I will give unto thee the keys of the kingdom of heaven: and whatsoever thou shalt bind on earth shall be bound in heaven: and whatsoever thou shalt loose on earth shall be loosed in heaven."[2] In fulfillment of this promise, Elijah passed the keys of the sealing power to Peter, James, and John when he and Moses appeared to the Savior on the Mount of Transfiguration.

In both instances, the purpose for the restoration of this sealing power was the same: to overcome apostasy. The Israelites had gone into apostasy during the four hundred years prior to the Lord's first coming; after the Lord's crucifixion and the deaths of His Apostles, the people again fell away and the Dark Ages began, not to be dispersed until the Restoration of all things in the latter days.

Sealing Ordinances

Just as the ordinance of sacrifice was performed outside the confines of a temple from the time of Adam until the reign of King Solomon, so also the sealing ordinances of the temple can be performed outside temples until one is constructed. So it was that the first sealing ordinance—baptism for the dead—was initially performed in the Mississippi River.

On October 19, 1840, Joseph wrote the following epistle to the Twelve as they labored in the British Mission:

> I presume the doctrine of "baptism for the dead" has ere this reached your ears, and may have raised some inquiries in your minds respecting the same.... I would say that it was certainly practiced by the ancient churches; and St. Paul endeavors to prove the doctrine of the resurrection from the same, and says, "Else what shall they do

---

2   Matthew 16:19.

which are baptized for the dead, if the dead rise not at all? Why are they then baptized for the dead?[3]

Joseph first mentioned the subject of baptism for the dead at the funeral of Seymour Brunson, who died on August 10, 1840.[4] The talk at Brother Brunson's

> Joseph Smith received revelation about baptism for the dead prior to 1840.

funeral was not recorded, but the fact that Joseph mentioned in his journal that this was the first public announcement of the ordinance would indicate that he had received a revelation on the doctrine prior to that time and had undoubtedly taught it privately to other members of the Church. His letter to the Twelve went on to say:

> The Saints have the privilege of being baptized for those of their relatives who are dead, whom they believe would have embraced the Gospel, if they had been privileged with hearing it, and who have received the Gospel in the spirit, through the instrumentality of those who have been commissioned to preach to them while in prison.[5]

The latter comment concerning spirits preaching to individuals held in a "prison" stems from the scriptural teaching of Peter:

> For Christ also hath once suffered for sins, the just for the unjust, that he might bring us to God, being put to death in the flesh, but quickened by the Spirit:
> By which also he went and preached unto the spirits in prison . . .

---

3   HC 2:231.

4   HC 4:179.

5   HC 4:231.

For for this cause was the gospel preached also to them that are dead, that they might be judged according to men in the flesh, but live according to God in the spirit.[6]

Joseph gave further instructions on this doctrine through a revelation he received from the Lord (now recorded in Section 124 of the Doctrine and Covenants)[7] and through an epistle he penned to the Saints while he was incarcerated in Liberty Jail.[8] Thus, baptism for the dead commenced in the Mississippi River and continued to be performed in the river until October 2, 1841, when the Lord commanded that it henceforth must be performed in the font of the Nauvoo Temple.[9]

| Baptism for the dead commenced in the Mississippi River.

A temporary baptismal font was dedicated in the basement of the temple on November 8, 1841, until "a more durable one [could] supply its place."[10] It was made of wood and sat upon twelve oxen representing the twelve tribes of Israel, which were also carved out of "pine planks, glued together, and copied after the most beautiful five-year-old steer that could be found in the country." The oxen and the ornamental moldings of the font took eight months to complete and were carved by Elijah Fordham. The water for the font was provided from a well thirty feet deep at the east end of the basement. The performance of baptism for the dead has continued in all LDS temples since that time.

The Endowment
The endowment that is now performed in all temples

6   1 Peter 3:18-20; 4:5-6.

7   D&C 124:29, 39. It was also in Section 124 that Joseph was commanded to build a "house" or temple to the Lord. See D&C 124:27.

8   D&C 127-128.

9   HC 4:426.

10   A complete description of the temporary baptismal font is found in the *History of the Church* 4:446.

built by the Church was first mentioned by the Prophet on May 4, 1842. It was introduced in Joseph's office, which was located on an upper story of his store in Nauvoo, Illinois. It was in this office that Joseph kept his sacred writings, translated ancient records, and received revelations.[11]

On this particular May day, Joseph recorded that he and several of the brethren had met together so that he could instruct "them in the principles and order of the Priesthood." He then mentioned that it included "washings, anointings, endowments and the communication of keys pertaining to the Aaronic Priesthood, and so on to the highest order of the Melchizedek Priesthood." In the records of this meeting, Joseph notes that he set forth . . .

Joseph first mentioned the endowment on May 4, 1842.

> . . . [T]he order pertaining to the Ancient of Days, and all those plans and principles by which any one is enabled to secure the fullness of those blessings which have been prepared for the Church of the First Born, and come up and abide in the presence of Eloheim in the eternal worlds. In this council was instituted the ancient order of things *for the first time in these last days.* And the communications I made to this council were of things spiritual, and to be received only by the spiritual minded: and there was nothing made known to these men but what will be made known to all the Saints of the last days, so soon as they are prepared to receive, and a proper place is prepared to communicate them, even to the weakest of the Saints . . . and wait their time with patience in all meekness, faith, [and] perseverance unto the

---

11   HC 5:1.

end, knowing assuredly that *all these things referred to in this council are always governed by the principle of revelation.*[12]

Two things are emphasized in the above paragraphs. First is the statement in the preceding quote that this was the first time the endowment had been introduced in the last days. (Some have questioned if the endowment was introduced earlier or if Joseph introduced it at all, suggesting that Brigham Young introduced it;[13] however, Joseph's personal diary clearly indicates the date the endowment was introduced, where it was introduced, and those who were the first to receive it.)[14] Second is the emphasis placed on the fact that the endowment itself was to be "governed by the principle of revelation." This also clearly indicates that changes to the endowment could be made, but only through revelation.

Historically, the endowment was suspended when the Saints left Illinois. The first endowment recorded thereafter occurred in the Salt Lake Valley on Ensign Hill (now Ensign Peak), on October 21, 1849. On that occasion, the endowment was given to Addison Pratt prior to his leaving on his mission.[15] The endowment was first committed to writing by Wilford Woodruff, who at the time was president of the St. George Temple. When the text was complete, it was presented to Brigham Young. He pronounced it correct and indicated that it would now serve as a model for all the temples.

The endowment used in LDS temples today differs somewhat from that introduced by Joseph Smith and recorded by Wilford Woodruff, although its function remains

---

12 HC 5:2. Emphasis added.

13 HC 5:2 ftnt, 3 ftnt.

14 The first members of the Church to receive their endowments were James Adams, Hyrum Smith, Newel K. Whitney, George Miller, Brigham Young, Heber C. Kimball, and Willard Richards (HC 5:1-30).

15 Roberts 3:386.

the same. Through revelation, minor changes have been made in wording and visual effects to enhance the presentation and make it more enjoyable for those participating. Although no details of the endowment will be given here due to its sacred nature, it can be noted that the ceremony primarily consists of a symbolic representation of the plan of salvation—from its presentation in the pre-existence and its role through the creation to the drama in the Garden of Eden. It culminates with the effects of Adam and Eve's transgression and portrays multiple relationships: the Father to His Son, the Father to mankind, the Son to mankind, the Son to the devil, mankind to the devil, men to women, etc.

The preliminaries to the endowment involve a washing and anointing that symbolically cleanses the body and the spirit from sin so that an individual can be accepted by the Lord and receive the blessings of the covenant of Abraham. The teachings of the endowment relate to our obedience to God, our agreement with the plan of salvation, and our desire to obey the commandments required to regain the Father's presence.

Throughout the ceremony, certain covenants are taken that allow the individual to commit to God's plan. These involve the laws of sacrifice, the gospel, chastity, and consecration and stewardship. The patron acknowledges acceptance of each of these laws as they are presented so that he or she is bound to them before the Lord. After completion of the endowment, the patron passes through the veil of the temple. This part of the ceremony represents the individual's acceptance by the Father and his or her entrance into His kingdom.

During the presentation of the endowment, the patron moves (either literally or by representation on film) through four rooms of the temple. Each room represents a stage in the plan of salvation. It begins with the Garden of Eden, then progresses through rooms representing the telestial world (or the world in which we now live) and the terrestrial world (or the return to the paradisaical existence of Eden). It culminates in the celestial world, the kingdom of God.

The purpose of the temple is to prepare righteous men and women | Temples prepare us for exaltation. for exaltation in the kingdom of God, where they will receive all the blessings the Father has to offer and become joint heirs with Jesus Christ.

Requirements for Entrance into the Lord's Temple

Only worthy members of The Church of Jesus Christ of Latter-day Saints can enter a temple once it has been dedicated.[16] Prior to their dedications, however, temples are open for a short period to allow visitors to tour their rooms and hear information concerning their purpose.

Once a temple is dedicated, worthy members who hold a temple recommend from their bishop or branch president (countersigned by a member of the appropriate stake or district presidency) are deemed worthy to enter the temple and participate in all of its ordinances. Males must hold the Melchizedek Priesthood. However, young men and women over the age of twelve can also enter the temple on a limited basis to be baptized for the dead. Again, their worthiness is determined in an interview with their bishop or branch president. In addition, young children and infants can enter the temple for the purpose of being sealed to their parents.

Applicants for temple recommends are asked several questions during a "recommend interview" by their bishop or branch president. Applicants are expected to answer the questions honestly before they can be determined worthy

---

16 There have been some exceptions to this rule. As mentioned in the chapter on temples, military officials and representatives of the Catholic Church entered the Nauvoo Temple after areas had been dedicated (these occurred after the death of the Prophet and before the Saints' exodus from Illinois). Today, individuals can enter for exigencies of government requirements and for emergency health or repair services.

to symbolically enter the presence of God. This is an honor system, but the priesthood leader conducting the interview is entitled to spiritual inspiration which may motivate him to pursue any one question in greater depth. The questions cover the following material:

- Whether applicants have a testimony of God the Father, His Son Jesus Christ, and the Holy Ghost, and if they have a conviction of the Savior's atonement and mission.

- Whether they have a testimony of the restoration of the gospel.

- Whether they sustain the President of the Church, and sustain the First Presidency and the Apostles as prophets, seers, and revelators.

- Whether they sustain other general authorities, as well as their own local authorities.

- Whether the applicants live the moral laws of the gospel and whether their family life is being conducted in harmony with the teachings of the Church.

- Whether the applicants have an affiliation with any apostate groups.

- Whether they are living in accordance with the covenants and teachings of the Church and regularly attend Church meetings.

- Whether they deal honestly with their associates, pay tithing, and live the Word of Wisdom.

- Whether they have any prior marital obligations and if so, whether they are honoring them.

- If the applicants have been to the temple previously, whether they are currently living according to temple requirements.

- Whether the applicants have any unresolved sins and finally, whether they feel they are worthy to enter the temple.

The Garment

During the process of receiving the endowment, a person is symbolically clothed in a special garment (underclothing) which he or she commits to wear throughout their lifetime. The garment is worn as a constant reminder of the covenants taken in the temple. It should be worn as normal underclothing twenty-four hours a day, but can be removed for such things as swimming, bathing, and exercising; or intensive sports like tennis, football, or basketball. During the temple recommend interview, members are reminded of the sacredness and purpose of the garment and their commitment to wear it appropriately.

Celestial Marriage

The phrase "celestial marriage" is not used in any of the revelations. It is a colloquialism that has developed through the years symbolizing the sacredness of the eternal relationship between husband and wife. This marriage ceremony (or sealing) is performed in the temple by authorized priesthood brethren who have been specifically set apart to do this work. (The ceremony can also be performed by any of the general authorities of the Church.)

Marriage sealings are only performed for those couples who have a legitimate marriage licence, or in the case of those who have been previously married civilly, a marriage certificate or verifiable, civilly recorded marriage date. The Church honors all marriages legally entered into under civil law, even though it seals that marriage in the temple under a separate ceremony and treats the couple being sealed as if this were their first marriage. (This same sealing ceremony is used for those standing proxy for the dead.)

A couple is sealed in marriage after they have received

their endowments. The ceremony is performed in a special room set aside for sealings where the couple kneels, facing each other across an altar. Most sealing rooms have large mirrors mounted on opposing walls that provide an aspect of eternity for the couple after they rise at the completion of the ceremony.

The sealing ceremony seals the couple not only for time, but for all eternity. It is a belief of the LDS Church that the family unit continues after death; therefore, the marriage relationship continues also.

Children born to a couple after they have been sealed in the temple are considered "born in the covenant," and no further temple ordinance work is done to ensure their eternal family relationship. However, if the couple has children as a result of a civil marriage or has adopted children, these children are sealed to the couple at the altars of the temple in a separate ceremony, again in the belief that the family unit continues after death.

All sealing ordinances can be performed by proxy for the dead within the sacred walls of the temple. They can be baptized, confirmed, ordained (in the case of men), washed and anointed, symbolically clothed in the garment of the holy priesthood, endowed, and sealed in marriage. They can also be sealed to their parents and to any children they may have had.

Temples are sacred. The restoration of the sealing power that functions within them—initially bestowed upon the Lord's chosen Apostles during His ministry—is a powerful evidence of the Restoration. It is important that the sanctity of the temples and the ordinances performed therein be maintained, not only while individuals are attending the temples, but throughout the activities of their daily lives.

PROSELYTING HELPS

The sealing power of the priesthood was held by the apostles and prophets of old, but it was taken from the earth during the Great Apostasy. Its restoration in the latter days is an obvious evidence of the restoration of the gospel.

- The ordinances performed in temples today require the sealing authority of the priesthood. These ordinances include baptism, the endowment, and sealings (including marriage for time and eternity).

- The prophet Elijah appeared to Joseph Smith and Oliver Cowdery on April 3, 1836, in the Kirtland Temple and restored the keys to the sealing power of the priesthood, thus fulfilling the prophecy found in Malachi 4:4–6.

- The scriptures reveal that baptism for the dead was practiced in New Testament times. In a letter to the Twelve Apostles in October of 1840, Joseph Smith stated that (thanks to the Restoration) the Latter-day Saints could also be baptized by proxy for their dead.

- To enter the temple, individuals must live lives in accordance with the Lord's commandments and qualify for a temple "recommend" issued by their bishop or branch president.

Temples are sacred. Ordinances performed and covenants taken therein should be honored during a person's daily activities and throughout their lives. If the person remains faithful, the LDS Church believes that the sealing power of the priesthood allows marriages and family units to continue past death. This knowledge is a great comfort to the Saints during times of bereavement and is often of interest to their nonmember friends who see the potential for their own families.

SECTION IV

Doctrinal Evidences

And Jesus, when he was baptized, went up straightway out of the water: and, lo, the heavens were opened unto him, and he saw the Spirit of God descending like a dove, and lighting upon him: [a]nd lo a voice from heaven, saying, This is my beloved Son, in whom I am well pleased.

Matthew 3:16–17

The Godhead

The true nature of the Godhead was lost to mankind's understanding after the councils of Nicaea and Constantinople, circa A.D. 325–381. It took the restoration of the gospel to again understand that the Godhead is composed of three separate and distinct individuals.

When Joseph wrote the Wentworth letter briefly explaining the origin and history of the Church, he concluded it with what has become known as the "Articles of Faith." They are not a Church *creed*, but rather a brief enumeration of some of the basic principles and doctrines of the Church. The first article states: "We believe in God, the Eternal Father, and in His Son, Jesus Christ, and in the Holy Ghost."[1] Every other Christian church of Joseph's time would have agreed with that statement; however, they did not agree

---

1   Articles of Faith 1:1.

with the Church's understanding of the *nature* of those three Gods.

The Christian churches of Joseph's day (and most Christian churches today) believed that the trinity of the Godhead was a three-in-one, mysterious, incomprehensible, noncorporeal entity. In one form or another, they believed in the description of God established by the Council of Nicaea circa A.D. 325 and refined by the Council of Constantinople circa A.D. 381.[2] From these creeds, we learn that they believed in "one God" which in some mysterious way comprised the Father, the Son, and the Holy Ghost: just one holy entity with three personalities. But as Jeffrey R. Holland noted in the November 2007 *Liahona*, "the stalwart *Harper's Bible Dictionary* records that 'the formal doctrine of the Trinity as it was defined by the great church councils of the fourth and fifth centuries is *not* to be found in the

---

2   *Creed from the Council of Nicaea circa A.D. 325:* "We believe in one God, the Father almighty, maker of all things visible and invisible; and in one Lord Jesus Christ, the Son of God, begotten from the Father, only-begotten, that is, from the substance of the Father, God from God, light from light, true God from true God, begotten not made, of one substance with the Father, through Whom all things came into being, things in heaven and things on earth, Who because of us men and because of our salvation, came down and became incarnate, becoming man, suffered and rose again on the third day, ascended into heaven, and will come to judge the living and the dead; And in the Holy Spirit.
    "But as for those who say, there was when He was not, and, before being born He was not, and that He came into existence out of nothing, or, who assert that the Son of God is of a different hypostasis or substance, or is created, or is subject to alteration or change—these the Catholic Church anathematizes" (CE IV: 435).
    Creed from the Council of Constantinople circa A.D. 381: "We believe in one God, the Father almighty, maker of heaven and earth, of all things visible and invisible; and in one Lord Jesus Christ, the only begotten Son of God, begotten from the Father before all ages, light from light, true God from true God, begotten not made, of one substance with the Father, through Whom all things came into existence; Who because of our salvation came down from heaven, and was incarnate from the Holy Spirit and the Virgin Mary and became man, and was crucified for us under Pontius Pilate, and suffered and was buried, and rose again on the third day according to the Scriptures, and ascended to heaven, and sits on the right hand of the Father, and will come again with glory to judge living and dead, of Whose kingdom there will be no end; and in the Holy Spirit, the Lord and life-giver, Who proceeds from the Father, Who with the Father and the Son is together worshipped and together glorified, Who spoke through the prophets; in one holy Catholic and apostolic Church. We confess one baptism to the remission of sins; we look forward to the resurrection of the dead, and the life of the world to come. Amen" (CE IV: 435).

[New Testament].' . . . If one says we are not Christians because we do not hold a fourth- or fifth-century view of the Godhead, then what of those first Christian Saints, many of whom were eyewitnesses of the living Christ, who did not hold such a view either?"

In Joseph Smith's first vision, he saw two separate and distinct beings—the Father and the Son—who were both in the form of a man. Later, the Prophet described what he had seen in writing: "The Father has a body of flesh and bones as tangible as man's; the Son also; but the Holy Ghost has not a body of flesh and bones, but is a personage of Spirit. Were it not so, the Holy Ghost could not dwell in us."[3] This concept of God was revolutionary, but it was not the only revolutionary doctrine about God that Joseph would reveal. In a Church Conference held on April 7, 1844, he delivered what has become known as the "King Follett Sermon" (King Follett was a worker who was killed during the construction of the Nauvoo Temple). His sermon covered many topics, but his initial subject concerned the nature and character of God. He began by declaring: "There are but a very few beings in the world who understand rightly the character of God. The great majority of mankind do not comprehend anything, either that which is past, or that which is to come, as it respects their relationship to God . . . consequently they know but little above the brute beast." He then asked the question. "What kind of a being is God?"[4]

After asking this question, Joseph turned to the scriptures and quoted from Chapter 17 of John: ". . . this is life eternal, that they might know thee the only true God, and Jesus Christ, whom thou has sent."[5] Continuing, he stated, "If any man does not know God, . . . if the declaration of

---

3   D&C 130:22.

4   HC 6:303.

5   John 17:3.

Jesus and the apostles be true, he will realize that he has not eternal life; for there can be eternal life on no other principle."[6] Speaking as one having authority, he then revealed the following truths:

> God himself was once as we are now, and is an exalted man, and sits enthroned in yonder heavens! That is the great secret. If the veil were rent today, and the great God who holds this world in its orbit, and who upholds all worlds and all things by His power, was to make himself visible,—I say, if you were to see him today, you would see him like a man in form—like yourselves in all the person, image, and very form as a man; for Adam was created in the very fashion, image and likeness of God, and received instruction from, and walked, talked and conversed with Him, as one man talks and communes with another.[7]

Joseph explained to the congregation of more than twenty thousand "how God came to be God," declaring again that God was "once a man like us; yea, that God himself, the Father of us all, dwelt on an earth, the same as Jesus Christ Himself did,"[8] and that the Saints must "learn how to be gods and to be kings and priests to God, the same as all gods have done before you."[9]

In another sermon delivered on June 16, 1844, Joseph continued the subject of the plurality of gods and the Godhead. He chose this subject because of the apostate accusation that he was a fallen prophet who taught and believed

---

6   HC 6:304.

7   HC 6:305.

8   HC 6:305.

9   HC 6:306.

in the plurality of gods. His chosen text was Revelation 1:6, which states: "And [Jesus Christ] hath made us kings and priests unto God and His Father: to Him be glory and dominion forever and ever. Amen." There are many other scriptures that discuss the plurality of gods, such as Psalm 32:1 ("God standeth in the congregation of the mighty; he judgeth among the gods") and Genesis 1:26 (". . . Let us make man in *our* image, after *our* likeness . . . [emphasis added]").

Joseph continued his sermon by stating, "I have always declared God to be a distinct personage, Jesus Christ a separate and distinct personage from God the Father, and that the Holy Ghost | God the Father; His Son, Jesus Christ; and the Holy Ghost comprise the Godhead.

was a distinct personage and a Spirit: and these three constitute three distinct personages and three Gods. . . . Many men say there is one God; the Father, the Son and the Holy Ghost are only one God! I say that is a strange God anyhow—three in one, and one in three!"[10] He concluded his discussion on the Godhead by asking, "Where was there ever a son without a father? And where was there ever a father without first being a son? Whenever did a tree or anything spring into existence without a progenitor? . . . Hence if Jesus had a Father, can we not believe that *He* had a Father also? I despise the idea of being scared to death at such a doctrine, for the Bible is full of it."[11]

Many scriptures from the Bible support the Prophet's depiction of the Godhead. Paul makes a distinction between Christ and the Father in Romans 8:34: ". . . It is Christ that died, yea rather, that is risen again, who is even at the right hand of God, who also maketh intercession for us." Another example is found in Hebrews 1:1–3 where the nature of God and Christ are discussed:

---

10   HC 6:476.

11   HC 6:476.

"God, who at sundry times and in divers manners spake in time past unto the fathers by the prophets,

Hath in these last days spoken unto us by his Son, whom he hath appointed heir of all things, by whom also he made the worlds;

Who being the brightness of his glory, and the express image of his person, and upholding all things by the word of his power, when he had by himself purged our sins, sat down on the right hand of the Majesty on High."

Christ also stated the individuality of the Godhead in John 14:26 : "But the Comforter, which is the Holy Ghost, whom the Father will send in my name, he shall teach you all things, and bring all things to your remembrance. . . ." And again in John 6:38, perhaps the best scripture to delineate between the Father and the Son, Christ simply states, "For I came down from heaven, not to do mine own will, but the will of him that sent me."

The scriptures also provide physical evidence of the individuality of the Godhead. In John 12:27–30, Jesus pled with His Father and His Father comforted Him: "Now is my soul troubled; and what shall I say? Father, save me from this hour: but for this cause came I unto this hour. Father, glorify thy name. Then came a voice from heaven, saying, I have both glorified it, and will glorify it again." Would Christ have prayed to Himself? Then answered Himself? Likewise, on the occasion of Christ's baptism and again on the Mount of Transfiguration, God the Father spoke from heaven to His Son, and in these cases others witnessed the events.[12]

One final evidence. In the Lord's great intercessory

---

12   Matthew 3:17; 17:5.

prayer,[13] He prayed that His Apostles would be one, as He and the Father were one.[14] At first glance, this statement might seem to affirm that the Father and the Son are one being. If we presume them to be one being, we must also presume that the Twelve could somehow merge into one being. Is it not more logical to understand that Christ and the Father are one in purpose? That they are united in their function and their endeavors, as are the Apostles?

Joseph Smith was teaching more than a new concept of the Godhead—he was describing a different God than that taught by other Christian religions. This brought condemnation upon both Joseph and the Church, and continues to be the basis for the claim that The Church of Jesus Christ of Latter-day Saints is not a Christian church.

PROSELYTING HELPS

The first article of faith says, "We believe in God, the Eternal Father, and in His Son, Jesus Christ, and in the Holy Ghost." Every other Christian church at the time of Joseph Smith would have agreed with that statement, but they did not agree with the Saints' understanding of the nature of those three Gods.

- The Nicaean and Constantinople councils defined the Godhead as one combined being. The subsequent creed—the Nicaean Creed—developed from that definition is the basis for most Christian Churches' doctrine of the Godhead.

- The LDS Church believes that the Godhead comprises

---

13   John 17.
14   John 17:21.

three distinct individuals: the Father; His Son, Jesus Christ; and the Holy Ghost.

- Joseph Smith saw God the Father and Jesus Christ. He stands as a witness that they are two distinct beings.

- The Father has a body of flesh and bones, as tangible as man's; the Son also; but the Holy Ghost does not have a body of flesh and bones, but is a personage of Spirit.

- This belief in "plural" gods is the basis for many claims that the LDS Church is not a Christian religion.

The New Testament has many references to God the Father as a unique being, separate from Jesus Christ. We can use these references, many from the Savior himself, to help nonmembers understand the true nature of God. Understanding the nature of God is the first step to teaching the plan of salvation and the role of Jesus Christ in that plan.

As we teach these things, we will help others to understand their relationship to God as a loving Father and to Jesus Christ as their Savior.

*And that repentance and remission of sins
should be preached in his name among
all nations, beginning at Jerusalem.*

Missionary Work

Missionary work is one of the requirements
of the Restoration. Without it, the Lord's goal
of salvation for mankind would be severely
constrained.

Just prior to His ascension, the Lord commanded His Apostles to "Go ye therefore, and teach all nations, baptizing them in the name of the Father, and of the Son, and of the Holy Ghost: Teaching them to observe all things whatsoever I have commanded you: and, lo, I am with you alway[s], even unto the end of the world. Amen."[1] It follows, therefore, that missionary work is one of the requirements of the Restoration, a requirement that applies to the Apostles of the latter days just as it did to Christ's Apostles of old.

Starting with the first Apostles called during the Restoration, the Twelve have been sustained as prophets, seers, revelators, and special witnesses to all nations of the

> Apostles today are sustained as prophets, seers, revelators, and special witnesses to all nations of the earth.

---

1   Matthew 28:19–20.

earth, "holding the keys of the kingdom, to unlock it, or cause it to be done, among them. . . ."[2] After the initial Twelve were sustained by the Saints in the Kirtland Temple, they were informed that among other things, they were required to obtain a personal testimony of Jesus Christ and bear it to the world. This is a requirement of all Apostles called in the latter days. They are the "Traveling High Council" of the Church, and are "to preside over the churches of the Saints, among the Gentiles, where there is a presidency established; and they are to travel and preach among the Gentiles, until the Lord shall command them to go to the Jews. They are to hold the keys of this ministry, to unlock the door of the kingdom of heaven unto all nations, and to preach the Gospel to every creature. This is the power, authority, and virtue of their apostleship."[3]

The Beginnings of Modern Missionary Work

Missionary work commenced in the restored Church even before the Twelve were called. Samuel Smith, Joseph's brother, was called on a mission on June 30, 1830. He took several copies of the Book of Mormon and proceeded to travel, attempting to sell them. During his trip, he was treated poorly by an innkeeper who not only refused to buy a copy of the book, but after hearing that it had been translated from gold plates, cursed at Samuel and commanded, "get out of my house—you shan't stay one minute with your books." Samuel was forced to sleep under an apple tree that night, some five miles further down the road. The next morning he knocked on the door of a nearby farm house belonging to the Reverend John P. Greene. The Reverend would not buy a book, but Samuel left a copy anyway.

Two weeks later, Samuel and his parents returned to the area of the inn only to find that smallpox had attacked the house infecting only the innkeeper and two of his fam-

---

2   HC 2:417.

3   HC 2:200.

ily. All three died. The book he left at the home of Reverend Greene, however, ultimately ended up in the possession of Brigham Young and Heber C. Kimball. Because of its message, both men were converted and eventually became two of the first Apostles of the Restoration.[4]

Approximately six months after the Church was organized, the Lord called for the first Lamanite Mission to be organized. As the title page of the Book of Mormon declares, the book is "Written

> The first mission was organized within six months of the Church's organization.

to the Lamanites, who are a remnant of the house of Israel," as well as to the Jews and the Gentiles. Consequently, in September of 1830 the Lord commanded Oliver Cowdery to "go unto the Lamanites and preach my gospel unto them."[5] At the September 26, 1830, conference of the Church, another revelation was received instructing Peter Whitmer, Jun., to go with Oliver Cowdery as his companion.[6] A later revelation called Parley P. Pratt and Zeba Peterson to accompany them.[7]

Parley P. Pratt had been a member of the Church for less than a month when he received this mission call. He had originally joined the "Disciples," a church started by Sidney Rigdon in Ohio (the Disciples were a break off from Alexander Campbell's "Campbellite" group). Upon joining the Disciples, Elder Pratt decided to become one of its ministers and left for New York to begin his ministry among his relatives. On the way, he heard about the Book of Mormon and sent his wife ahead to his family while he diverted to Palmyra to investigate. There he met Hyrum Smith, and together they traveled to Fayette, New York, to see Oliver Cowdery. After a short visit with Oliver, Elder Pratt was baptized in Seneca Lake and ordained an Elder. He proceeded on to his family in Columbia County, New

---

4   HC 7:216-218.

5   D&C 28:8-10; HC 1:111.

6   D&C 30:5-6.

7   D&C 32.

York, where he baptized his nineteen-year-old brother, Orson Pratt. Then he returned to Fayette to the conference and received his mission call to the Lamanites.[8]

Shortly thereafter, four of the brethren left Fayette, New York, to go into the "wilderness" to teach the gospel.[9] They traveled first to the Catteraugus tribe near Buffalo, New York. They spent some time preaching to the members of that tribe and left two copies of the Book of Mormon with those who could read English. They then continued westward to Mentor, Ohio, a short distance from Kirtland, where they met Sidney Rigdon.[10]

Sidney Rigdon was a "Regular Baptist" initially, but was later involved with Alexander Campbell, founder of the Campbellites and its break off, the Disciples. When Sidney heard the gospel, he invited Oliver and Parley to preach to his congregation and encouraged the membership to thoughtfully consider the things they had to say. Sidney studied the Book of Mormon and after a fortnight, concluded that the work was true. Shortly thereafter, he and his wife were baptized.

During Sidney's period of reflection and study, however, the four missionaries traveled on to Kirtland and met with many of Sidney's congregation living in that area. After teaching them the gospel and bearing their testimonies to them, seventeen men and women joined the Church. They also baptized Frederick G. Williams and left behind them a newly organized branch of twenty members. Thereafter they departed, "bound for the borders of the Lamanites."[11]

The missionaries next traveled to the Wyandot tribe near Sandusky, Ohio. They were well received and were told of other tribes that had already moved to Indian Territory further west. They then continued on to Indepen-

---

8   HC 1:118 ftnt, 119 ftnt.

9   D&C 32; HC 1:120.

10   HC 1:120 ftnt, 121 ftnt.

11   HC 1:124-125 & ftnt.

dence, Missouri, and surrounding areas where the Delaware Tribe was located. During this time, they were able to meet with Chief Anderson of the Delawares. Although they were initially received with caution, the chief eventually called a council meeting and allowed the brethren to preach. He responded well to a speech Oliver Cowdery delivered, and the brethren were able to teach for several days. Several members of the tribe were subsequently converted and baptized.

In June of 1837—after the severe persecutions sustained in Ohio and Missouri—Joseph received another revelation pertaining to missionary work. He recorded the following in his journal: "God revealed to me that something new must be done for the salvation of His Church." As a result, the Prophet contacted Heber C. Kimball and set him apart "by the spirit of prophecy and revelation, prayer and laying on of hands, of the First Presidency, to preside over a mission to England, to be the first foreign mission of the Church of Christ in the last days."[12] The opening of the British Mission was a momentous undertaking for the Saints and resulted in many interesting stories, a few of which are related here.

> The first foreign mission was opened in 1837.

Departure to the British Mission

On July 8, 1838, the Prophet Joseph Smith asked the Lord to show the Saints His will concerning the affairs of the Twelve. The Lord responded with what is now Section 118 of the Doctrine and Covenants. In that revelation, the Twelve were commanded to "depart to go over the great waters." They were to leave from the city of Far West on April 26, 1839, from the "building-spot" designated for the Lord's temple.

Prior to this prophesied departure, Joseph was arrested

---

12   HC 2:489.

and put in jail and the Saints were driven from the state of Missouri under Governor Boggs' Extermination Order. However, when April 26, 1839, approached, the Apostles left Illinois and secretly made their way to Far West, Missouri, arriving shortly after midnight on the 26th. They silently approached the site that had been dedicated for the temple and Alpheus Cutler, the "master workman of the house," rolled a large stone close to where the southeast corner of the temple foundation was scheduled to be laid. After this was accomplished, the Twelve proceeded to quietly reorganize the Quorum. They sustained and ordained several new members to replace those who had been excommunicated during the Missouri persecutions, softly sang the song, "Adam-ondi-Ahman," took their leave of those who had attended the meeting, and returned to Quincy, Illinois. Joseph recorded the following in his journal: "Thus was fulfilled a revelation of July 8, 1838, which our enemies had said could not be fulfilled, as no 'Mormon' would be permitted to be in the state."[13]

Brigham Young and Heber C. Kimball finally left for England on September 14, 1839, under extremely trying circumstances, as the *History of the Church* indicates:

> President Brigham Young started from his home at Montrose, for England. His health was very poor; he was unable to go thirty rods to the river without assistance. After he had crossed the ferry he got Brother Israel Barlow to carry him on his horse behind him to Heber C. Kimball's where he remained sick until the 18th. He left his wife sick with a babe only ten days old, and all his children sick, unable to wait upon each other.[14]
>
> Elder Kimball left his wife in bed shak-

---

13   HC 3:336-339.
14   HC 4:9.

ing with ague [a feverish illness, usually malarial, with recurring chills], and all his children sick. It was only by the assistance of some of the brethren that Heber himself could climb into the wagon. 'It seemed to me,' he remarked afterwards in relating the circumstance, 'as though my very inmost parts would melt within me at the thought of leaving my family in such a condition, as it were, almost in the arms of death. I felt as though I could scarcely endure it.' 'Hold up!' said he to the teamster, who had just started, 'Brother Brigham, this is pretty tough, but let us rise and give them a cheer.' Brigham, with much difficulty, rose to his feet, and joined Elder Kimball in swinging his hat and shouting, 'Hurrah, hurrah, hurrah, for Israel!' The two sisters, hearing the cheer came to the door—Sister Kimball with great difficulty—and waved a farewell; and the two apostles continued their journey, without purse, without scrip, for England.[15]

Most of these brethren's travels from Nauvoo to New York were overland; however, at one point they boarded the steamer *Columbus,* to travel from Fairport to Buffalo. On the morning of November 27, 1839, a wind arose that was so strong it caused Brigham Young to leave his stateroom, go on deck, and pray that the wind and waves would cease so that they could proceed safely on their journey. "The winds abated, and he gave glory, honor, and praise to God who rules all things."[16]

When Brigham and Heber finally set sail for England,

---

15   HC 4:9 ftnt, 10 ftnt.

16   HC 4:23.

they were still in very poor health. The Saints living in the area came to the dock and bid them bon voyage by singing, "The gallant ship is under weigh."[17] But sailing did nothing to alleviate their illness. They had been at sea only twelve hours when "the whole of them were prostrated by sea-sickness." Brigham Young was confined to his berth the entire journey. When they finally arrived at their destination, "Brother Young shouted hosanna three times, which he had promised to do whenever he should land on the shores of Old England."[18] It goes without saying that he was undoubtedly grateful to be on terra firma once more.

The Apostles were almost penniless when they arrived in England. A few had sufficient funds to buy hats for some of the brethren who needed them most. When they arrived in Preston by train, they did not have "a single sixpence left."[19] But the Lord assisted the brethren in their time of need—ways and means were provided—and they embarked on an incredible mission that would eventually bring thousands into the Church.[20]

Thousands of people joined the Church in England.

---

17   HC 4:103.

18   HC 4:104.

19   HC 4:105, 111.

20   Among the thousands of baptisms performed in England, one unique occurrence demonstrates that baptism cannot be taken lightly. Unbeknownst to his wife, Thomas Cartwright was baptized by Elder Jonathan Pugmire, Senior, on November 6, 1843. Suspicious of her husband's absence, Mrs. Cartwright went to the home of Elder Pugmire and inquired of his wife where her husband was. Sister Pugmire said she did not know. After leaving the house, Mrs. Cartwright met both her husband and Elder Pugmire returning from his baptism. She screamed at her husband, ". . . I'll dip ye!" followed by several expletives and threats of revenge on the Pugmire family. Several nonmember neighbors of the Pugmires witnessed the scene and warned Mrs. Cartwright not to speak against the Latter-day Saints since she might be converted to their church and be baptized herself one day. To this Mrs. Cartwright said, "I hope to God, if ever I am such a fool, that I'll be drowned in the attempt!" A short time later, as a result of her husband's conversations with her, she began attending meetings at the Pugmire home. Some weeks passed and she finally confessed her belief in the restored Church and expressed her desire to be baptized, noting that she had had a dream "in which she saw that it was a fearful thing to fall into the hands of the living God." She was embarrassed that so many people had heard her previous ranting against her husband's baptism and so requested that her baptism

Missionary Work Today

Since the inauguration of missionary work to the Lamanites and to the British Isles, the missionary | The gospel will be preached in every nation on earth.

program of the Church has been in continuous operation. As the Church has grown, the responsibility for doing missionary work—a task obviously too great for twelve men alone—has expanded to include all young men nineteen and older, single women twenty-one and older, and retired couples who are able to serve. In addition to these full-time missionaries, since the administration of President David O. McKay (1951–1970), the Church has declared "every member a missionary."[21]

Today, the Church is putting great emphasis on member participation in missionary work. Each baptized member is asked to seek opportunities to share the gospel with nonmembers and inactive members alike. In doing so, they fulfill their responsibility within the covenant of Abraham to take the gospel to all the world, and comply with the revelation in Doctrine and Covenants 88:81–82 which states: "Behold, I send you out to testify and warn the people, and it becometh every man who hath been warned

---

be done in private. Only James Moore, Elder and Sister Pugmire, and her husband were asked to be present. On the evening of November 23, 1843, they started for the banks of a stream in which Elder Pugmire had baptized eight or ten persons earlier in the day. Upon their arrival, they found that the rain during the day had caused the stream to rise over its banks. Elder Pugmire waded into the water and decided that he could baptize Mrs. Cartwright without going into the regular bed of the steam. He took Mrs. Cartwright into the water and baptized her, but upon raising her from the water, the bank gave way and they both disappeared into the torrent. With the help of Mrs. Pugmire, James Moore got hold of Elder Pugmire by the hair and dragged him out of the water. Mr. Cartwright caught hold of the petticoat of Mrs. Cartwright, but the petticoat came off and they were both swept away. Mr. Cartwright was found about a hundred yards downstream holding onto the stump of a tree and was rescued. Mrs. Cartwright was not found until the next day. She was discovered "about two hundred yards from where the accident occurred, standing upon her feet, with her head above water, the stream having fallen about two feet." She was, of course, dead. Both Mr. Cartwright and Elder Pugmire were arrested and spent six weeks and three days in jail, but they were acquitted at their trial. The judge merely warned them that they should be more cautions when selecting a site to hold baptisms (HC 6:160-162).

21 Conference Report, April 1959, 122.

to warn his neighbor. Therefore, [when they are warned] they are left without excuse, and their sins are upon their own heads."

Starting with the Savior's original Twelve Apostles, at one time or another the gospel has now been proselyted in many nations and is fulfilling the prophecy of Daniel concerning the little stone (the gospel) that would be cut out of the mountain and roll forth to fill the whole earth.[22]

PROSELYTING HELPS

The requirement of "every member a missionary" is as applicable today as it was in the days of Joseph Smith. To be a missionary today is to be part of the proud heritage established by men and women who have worked tirelessly through the years to spread the gospel on the Lord's behalf.

- Starting with the Lord's Apostles (who are sustained as prophets, seers, revelators, and special witnesses to all the nations of the earth), individuals have the opportunity and the obligation to serve as missionaries, either formally or informally.

- The first Church mission (the Lamanite Mission) was established less than six months after the Church was organized. Missionary work is obviously one of the Lord's priorities.

- The first foreign mission was opened in 1837. Brethren were sent to England to proselyte and as a result, thousands of individuals came into the Church in a short period of time.

---

22   Daniel 2:35.

- Today, the gospel has been proselyted in many nations throughout the earth.

Missionary work is a biblically based responsibility to all those who have received the truth. Every faithful member of the Church of Jesus Christ of Latter-day Saints is cognizant of the need to spread the gospel. We live in the last days, and it is the last time the Lord will offer the gospel of salvation to the people of the earth. But members of the Church are often asked why we do missionary work, especially among other Christians. The answer is simple. Many important principles and ordinances of the gospel of Jesus Christ, necessary for salvation, were lost during the Great Apostasy. But as the evidences herein have shown, the fullness of Christ's true church has been restored to the earth. Therefore, members of the LDS Church have a responsibility to share those restored principles and ordinances with all people (adding to whatever truth they may already have), thereby allowing all God's children the opportunity to receive exaltation.

Hear, ye children, the instruction of a father,
and attend to know understanding. For I give
you good doctrine, forsake ye not my law.

Proverbs 4:1–2

Doctrinal Integrity

Doctrinal integrity is essential for the exaltation of mankind. False or distorted doctrines will not get anyone into the Father's kingdom.

One of the principal reasons the epistles of the New Testament were written was to correct doctrinal errors that were creeping into the new branches of the early church. Because communication at that time was so difficult, doctrinal integrity was hard to maintain. Once it was lost, the doctrines had to be restored again in their purity; this occurred during the Restoration when the gospel was restored to the Prophet Joseph Smith, one precept at a time.

The Kingdom of God

On Sunday, January 22, 1843, Joseph delivered a sermon on the topic, "The Kingdom of God." The selection of the topic came about through some questions that had been posed to him during the previous week. He opened the sermon by stating that some said the kingdom of God did not come upon the earth until the day of Pentecost when the Apostles received the Holy Ghost. But Joseph disagreed with this. He stated that the kingdom of God "was set up on the earth from the days of Adam to the present time."[1] He elaborated on this statement by adding:

> Whenever there has been a righteous man on earth unto whom God revealed His word and gave power and authority to administer in His name, and where there is a priest of God—a minister who has power and authority from God to administer in the ordinances of the gospel and officiate in the priesthood of God, there is the kingdom of God.[2]

In other words, in order to have the kingdom of God upon the earth, the following conditions must be met:

- There must be a righteous man on the earth.
- God must reveal his word and bestow on man His authority to act.
- The ordinances of the gospel must be revealed.

Joseph stated that without these conditions being in place, "there the kingdom of God is not."[3] He further noted that John the Baptist held the keys to the Aaronic Priesthood and Jesus held the keys to the Melchizedek Priesthood, concluding that, "all the ordinances, systems, and administrations on the earth are of no use to the children of men, unless they are ordained and authorized of God."[4]

The Word of Wisdom
After Moses led the children of Israel out of Egypt,

---

1   HC 5:256.
2   HC 5:256.
3   HC 5:257.
4   HC 5:259.

God gave him the rules and regulations (commandments) that the Israelites were to live by, declaring, "For thou art an holy people unto the Lord thy God, and the Lord hath chosen thee to be a peculiar people unto himself, above all the nations that are upon the earth."[5]

After he made this proclamation, Moses proceeded to recount the Israelites' basic law of health under the Mosaic code—what Chapter 14 of Deuteronomy connotes as a "word of wisdom." The Israelites were forbidden to eat pork or any animal that had a cloven foot but did not chew the cud; the rest of the chapter relates specific regulations that cover all types of food.

In the New Testament, Paul wrote about the importance of the physical body and the requirement to keep it clean:

> Know ye not that ye are the temple of God, and that the Spirit of God dwelleth in you?
>
> If any man defile the temple of God, him shall God destroy; for the temple of God is holy, which temple ye are.[6]
>
> What? Know ye not that your body is the temple of the Holy Ghost which is in you, which ye have of God, and ye are not your own?[7]

> The Word of Wisdom denotes the importance of the physical body in God's eyes.

These words of wisdom from Deuteronomy and 1 Corinthians are straightforward and explicit. They demand attention, command obedience, and promise rewards, yet they allow the observer the agency to choose if he or she will obey. Is it any wonder, then, that a word of wis-

---

5   Deuteronomy 14:2.

6   1 Corinthians 3:16-17.

7   1 Corinthians 6:19.

dom should be revealed to the Lord's people of the latter days? On August 7, 1831, He gave them a preview of this commandment:

> Yea, and the herb, and the good things which come of the earth, whether for food or for raiment, or for houses, or for barns, or for orchards, or for gardens, or for vineyards;
>
> Yea, all things which come of the earth, in the season thereof, are made for the benefit and use of man, both to please the eye and to gladden the heart;
>
> Yea, for food and for raiment, for taste and for smell, to strengthen the body and to enliven the soul.
>
> And it pleaseth God that he hath given all these things unto man; for unto this end were things made to be used, with judgment, not to excess, neither by extortion.[8]

It has been said that the problem of smoke-filled rooms and spit-covered floors resulting from the meetings Joseph held with the brethren (particularly meetings of the School of the Prophets in Kirtland) caused Emma Smith to confront the Prophet. Their use of chewing tobacco and pipes apparently created a mess she was loathe to clean up.

On February 13, 1833, and again on February 27, 1833, a council of high priests had assembled to investigate the proceedings of a man named Burr Riggs; it was to the brethren assembled at the second council meeting that the Word of Wisdom (as recorded in Section 89 of the Doctrine and Covenants) was specifically addressed. However, the first verse of Section 89 expands the application to "the church, and also the saints in Zion"—in other words, it is applicable to all members of the Church.

---

8   D&C 59:17-20.

Initially, the Word of Wisdom was given not by "commandment or constraint, but by revelation . . . showing forth the order and will of God." Some of the early members interpreted this to mean that they did not have to obey the commandment, but on April 6, 1838, in Far West, Missouri, Joseph stated that it was no longer a suggestion and "should be observed."[9]

One of the interesting things about this revelation is that the Lord declared it was "adapted to the capacity of the weak and the weakest of all saints, who are or can be called saints,"[10] and was given because of the "evils and designs which do and will exist in the hearts of conspiring men in the last days."[11]

Multiple things are forbidden in the Word of Wisdom:

- *Wine and strong drink* including all alcoholic beverages. Section 89 states that they are only good "for the washing of your bodies."[12]

- *Tobacco* is "an herb for bruises and all sick cattle, to be used with judgment and skill."[13]

- The Lord said *hot drinks* were not for the body or the belly. Some time after this revelation was given, Joseph clarified what hot drinks were: "I understand that some of the people are excusing themselves in using tea and coffee, because the Lord only said 'hot drinks' in the revelation of the Word of Wisdom. Tea and coffee are what the Lord meant when he said 'hot drinks.'"[14]

---

9   HC 3:15.

10   D&C 89:3.

11   D&C 89:4.

12   D&C 89:7.

13   D&C 89:8.

14   John A. and Leah D. Widtsoe, *The Word of Wisdom* (Salt Lake City: Deseret Book, 1938), 85.

By implication, the Word of Wisdom "do nots" would include any other substance that is harmful to the body (including, but not limited to, the misuse of drugs).

There are many things, however, that the Lord said are good for the body:

- Wholesome herbs in the season thereof.

- Every fruit in the season thereof.

- Flesh of beasts used sparingly and in times of winter or famine.

- All grain for the food of man. It is the staff of life. (The Lord also listed specific grains and their uses in this section.)

Punishment for disobedience of this commandment was more stringent in the early days of the Church than it is today. Joseph stated that "no official member in this Church is worthy to hold an office after having the Word of Wisdom properly taught him; and he, the official member, neglecting to comply with and obey it."[15] President Heber J. Grant said, "If a man thinks more of a cup of tea or coffee, or a cigarette, or a chew of tobacco than he does of his priesthood, let him resign his priesthood."[16] People were both disfellowshipped[17] and excommunicated for breaking the Word of Wisdom during Joseph's ministry:[18] the sacrament was not administered to them;[19] high priests were required to state whether they lived it or not;[20] and the Saints were admonished to not support those who sold items forbidden by the revelation.[21]

---

15   TPJS 117.

16   *Deseret Weekly News*, 6 October 1894, 50:1.

17   HC 2:482.

18   HC 2:218, 228.

19   HC 2:34.

20   HC 5:84.

21   HC 2:524.

However, the Lord promised choice blessings to those who would live the constraints contained in the Word of Wisdom. They would receive health in their navel and marrow to their bones; they would find wisdom and great treasures of knowledge, even hidden treasures; they would walk and not become weary; they would run and not faint; and the destroying angel would pass them by, as it had the children of Israel at the time of the Passover.[22] The Savior also made it clear in Section 89 that He had restored this code of health for the "temporal salvation of all saints in the last days."[23]

> The Lord's blessings are promised to those who live the Word of Wisdom.

The Gifts of the Spirit

There are three books of scripture that record a list of the gifts of the Spirit: the Bible,[24] the Book of Mormon,[25] and the Doctrine and Covenants.[26] The Lord gave these gifts to His people anciently, and He has given them to people today.

The book of Matthew initiates a discussion on the gifts of the Spirit with the story of Jesus and His Apostles on the coasts of Caesarea Philippi. The Lord had recently delivered His "bread of life" sermon where He had clearly claimed to be the Son of God.[27] The result of His sermon had been the defection of many of His disciples, for He had made it clear that His kingdom was spiritual and not of this earth. The disappointed Jews had been anticipating a strong temporal leader. Even the Twelve were bothered in their minds, and Jesus asked them, "Will ye

> Everyone has been given at least one of the gifts of the spirit.

22 D&C 89:18-21.
23 D&C 89:2.
24 1 Corinthians 12:4-11, 31.
25 Moroni 10:8-17.
26 D&C 46:10-29.
27 Sermons 104.

also go away?"[28] On an earlier occasion, the Pharisees and Sadducees had asked the Lord some difficult questions and again, His answers may have disappointed the Twelve, for He would not openly confront nor publically challenge the Jewish leaders. It apparently bothered the Apostles that the Savior was not measuring up to the Jews' expectations of their anticipated Messiah. With these experiences fresh in their minds, they silently set sail with the Lord to cross the Sea of Galilee.

In this private setting, Jesus asked the Twelve, "Whom do men say that I the Son of man am?" They responded that some thought He was Elijah, some Jeremiah, and others John the Baptist—not that He was the literal reincarnation of these great men, but that he was continuing their work in preparation for a Messiah yet to come. It is obvious that even though the Jews differed in their perceived purpose of Christ's mission, they still considered Him an extraordinary man with a mission from heaven.

Then Christ asked His Apostles, "But whom say ye that I am?" Peter boldly stepped forward, undoubtedly speaking for all the Twelve, and replied, "Thou art the Christ, the Son of the living God."

Although the three Synoptics disagree on the exact wording of Peter's reply, the meaning is the same: the Twelve knew at that point that Jesus was, in fact, the Son of God, the long-awaited Messiah and Savior of the world. Their belief was based on a confirmation from the Spirit, a gift sent by the Father, and the Savior confirmed this when He said, "Blessed art thou, Simon Barjona: for flesh and blood hath not revealed it unto thee, but my Father which is in heaven."[29]

In the Bible, Paul begins his teaching on the gifts of the Spirit in 1 Corinthians when he states, "Wherefore I give

---

28   John 6:67.
29   Matthew 16:13-28.

you to understand, that no man speaking by the Spirit of God calleth Jesus accursed: and that no man can say that Jesus is the Lord, but by the Holy Ghost."[30] In the Book of Mormon, Moroni discusses the gifts by declaring, ". . . by the power of the Holy Ghost ye may know the truth of all things . . . and they [the gifts of the Spirit] are given by the manifestations of the Spirit of God unto men, to profit them."[31] The description of the gifts of the Spirit in the Doctrine and Covenants states, "For all have not every gift given unto them; . . . To some is given one, and to some is given another, that all may be profited thereby. To some it is given by the Holy Ghost to know that Jesus Christ is the Son of God, and that he was crucified for the sins of the world. To others it is given to believe on their words, that they also might have eternal life if they continue faithful."[32]

The authors of these books of scripture all recite gifts that the Lord has given to mankind. A comparison of the three scriptural lists makes it evident that Paul was correct in Corinthians when he said, "Now there are diversities of gifts, but the same spirit."[33] While the references duplicate some gifts and describe others in different (but similar) words, it is obvious that all three prophets received their revelation from the same source.[34]

By eliminating the duplication in the scriptural lists, the following sixteen gifts are identified:

---

30   1 Corinthians 12:3.

31   Moroni 10:5, 8.

32   D&C 46:11–14.

33   1 Corinthians 12:4.

34   Gifts of the spirit are recounted in the scriptures as follows:
Bible (Paul's list): Testimony, diversity of administrations, diversities of operations, wisdom, knowledge, faith, healing, miracles, prophecy, discerning of spirits, diverse kinds of tongues, interpretation of tongues.
The Book of Mormon (Moroni's list): Testimony, administration of gifts, wisdom, knowledge, faith, gifts of healing, miracles, prophecy, beholding of angels, ministering spirits, interpretation of languages, diverse kinds of tongues.
The Doctrine and Covenants (Joseph Smith's list): Testimony, differences of administration, diversities of operations, wisdom, knowledge, faith to be healed, faith to heal, working of miracles, prophecy, discerning of spirits, speaking with tongues, interpretation of tongues.

1. Testimony
2. Diversity of administrations
3. Diversities of operations
4. Wisdom
5. Knowledge
6. Faith
7. Faith to be healed
8. Faith to heal
9. Miracles
10. Prophecy
11. Discerning of spirits
12. Speaking with tongues
13. Interpretation of tongues
14. Administration of gifts
15. Beholding of angels
16. Ministering spirits

Any reading of the Bible, the Book of Mormon, or the Doctrine and Covenants (as contained in the *History of the Church*) will exhibit the use or exercise of the gifts of the Spirit. These sources indicate that not all gifts are given to every man and woman, but that they all receive at least one gift: ". . . for there are many gifts, and to every man is given a gift by the Spirit of God."[35] It is a teaching the Lord himself gave in parable form when He recited the parables of the pounds and talents.[36] In the parable of the pounds, each individual was given the same amount to use—one pound—without taking the ability of the user into consideration. In the parable of the talents, the number of talents bestowed was commensurate with the individuals' ability to use them. Each of the parables indicates that the individuals' reward (or judgment) is based on how they use the gifts they have been given, which includes a punishment for not using them at all.

---

35   D&C 46:11.
36   Parables 101, 107.

Why are the gifts of the spirit an evidence of the Restoration? Because today they are an integral part of the gospel of Jesus Christ and are necessary to gain a testimony of the Godhead and of the gospel, just as they were anciently. Further, their very use is evidence that the gospel has been restored, that the Book of Mormon is true, and that the Spirit of God is again functioning upon the earth.

| Gifts of the spirit are an evidence of the Restoration.

Work for the Dead

Work for the dead was discussed at length in a previous chapter and it is not necessary to detail that work here, except to note that it is one of the most remarkable elements of the Restoration. You will recall that Elijah restored the keys of the sealing power to Joseph Smith and Oliver Cowdery in the Kirtland Temple, and these keys made it possible for this work to go forth in the last dispensation of time.

Jesus was the first to discuss the need of work for the dead. After He had healed the impotent man at the pool of Bethesda, He gave a sermon to the rulers who were questioning the fact that He was healing on the Sabbath. "Very, verily, I say unto you," He began. "The hour is coming, and now is, when the dead shall hear the voice of the Son of God: and they that hear shall live." His comment pertained to the judgment that would eventually come upon all who were deceased. He told the Jews, "Marvel not at this: for the hour is coming, in the which all that are in the graves shall hear [My] voice," to come forth either in the "resurrection of life" or in the "resurrection of damnation."[37]

| The doctrine of work for the dead is founded in the Bible.

After the Lord's resurrection, Paul mentioned this doctrine when he indicated to the Corinthians that some work

---

37   John 5:25-30.

for the dead had been performed after the early church had been established. "Else what shall they do which are baptized for the dead," he asked, "if the dead rise not at all? why are they then baptized for the dead?"[38] It is interesting to note that the Corinthians were performing this ordinance for the dead even though they had doubts about the resurrection itself, and Paul's logical argument pointed out this oxymoron.

Next, Peter confirmed what the Lord had taught concerning the reason for teaching the gospel to the dead—i.e., judgment. The gospel must be made available to all who live, will yet live, or who have lived upon the earth so that they can exercise their agency in either accepting or rejecting it. Peter stated, "For this cause was the gospel preached also to them that are dead, that they might be judged according to men in the flesh, but live according to God in the spirit."[39]

While we do not have complete information on work for the dead in the Bible and there is no mention of it at all in the Book of Mormon, the doctrine had to be restored in order to have a complete restoration of all things in the latter days. Now that it has been made available to those who hold the proper authority, Church members can do the work required for the salvation and exaltation of those who have gone before: baptism; confirmation; priesthood ordination for men; and temple work consisting of washing and anointing, the endowment, and sealing ordinances both for couples in marriage and for family groups.

The information on work for the dead was greatly expanded with the inclusion of President Joseph F. Smith's October 3, 1918, vision, as recorded in Section 138 of the Doctrine and Covenants. He had been pondering the scriptures in 1 Peter where the Lord "went and preached unto

---

38   1 Corinthians 15:29.

39   1 Peter 4:6.

the spirits in prison; Which sometime were disobedient"[40] when a vision opened to him and he saw the work that was being done in the spirit world between those who knew of the gospel and those who did not. From this vision, we learn that Jesus did not go personally to the spirits who had been wicked while they were on the earth, such as those who lived during the time of Noah. Rather, He went to the righteous spirits and organized those spirits as teaching missionaries who would go to the spirit prison and preach the gospel, thus fulfilling Peter's proclamation. This is the reason that work for the dead was performed after Christ's resurrection and why we perform it today: so that those who did not hear and/or obey the gospel in mortality will have the opportunity to hear and accept it in the spirit world and be judged according to men in the flesh. The vision states:

> The dead who repent will be redeemed, through obedience to the ordinances of the house of God [temple ordinances].
> And after they have paid the penalty of their transgressions, and are washed clean, shall receive a reward according to their works, for they are heirs of salvation.[41]

Work for the dead was and continues to be a major doctrinal concept that separates the Church of Jesus Christ of Latter-day Saints from all other Christian faiths. However, even with the limited references showing or alluding to work for the dead in biblical times, and the lack of understanding by Christian churches that developed during the Great Apostasy, it is obvious that the reestablishment of this work was necessary to complete the restoration of the gospel in the latter days.

---

40   1 Peter 3:18-20; 4:6.

41   D&C 138:58-59.

PROSELYTING HELPS

The epistles recorded in the New Testament were written to correct doctrinal errors that were creeping into the Lord's church. After Christ's ancient Apostles died, it was not long before doctrinal integrity was lost. The doctrines had to be restored so that salvation could be offered to mankind one last time. This occurred during the Restoration—one doctrine at a time.

- The kingdom of God exists whenever there is a righteous man on the earth who has been given power from God (priesthood authority) to administer the ordinances of the gospel.

- All ordinances, systems, and administrations on the earth are of no use to mankind unless they are ordained and authorized of God.

- The fact that the Lord gave us the Word of Wisdom evidences the importance of the physical body in God's eyes and the requirement to keep it clean—inside and out.

- The main focus of the Word of Wisdom as found in Section 89 of the Doctrine and Covenants is abstinence from the following: strong drinks (alcoholic beverages), tobacco in any form, hot drinks (later defined as tea and coffee by Joseph Smith), and by implication, any other substance that is harmful to the body (including, but not limited to, the misuse of drugs). Those foods that are beneficial to mankind are also discussed.

- The Lord's choicest blessings are promised to those who live the Word of Wisdom in its fullness.

- The Bible, the Book of Mormon, and the Doctrine and Covenants all list gifts of the Spirit (such things as wisdom, knowledge, faith, testimony, etc.). The parables of the pounds and the talents make it clear that everyone has been given at least one of these gifts and is responsible before the Lord to exercise it.

- Gifts of the spirit are an evidence of the Restoration because they are an integral part of the gospel and are necessary to gain a testimony of the Lord and His work.

- Work for the dead is one of the most remarkable elements of the Restoration. It is a major doctrine that separates the LDS Church from all other Christian faiths.

Once doctrinal purity had been reestablished through the Restoration of the gospel, the opportunity for exaltation was again available to mankind. This gives an even greater impetus to the need for missionary work. The Father wants all of His children to return to Him.

Many doctrines of the Church of Jesus Christ of Latter-day Saints are unique from any other church. However, they are all based on doctrines Christ established and can be substantiated by the Bible. When asked about these concepts, we can refer to the biblical references, pointing out that the concepts were lost during the Great Apostasy, but that the scriptures also foretold a restoration of all things.[42] Through the restoration of His true church in the latter days, the Lord has once again made all these things available to bless His people.

---

42   Ephesians 1:10.

SECTION V

Judgment and the Kingdoms Of Glory

*For the Father judgeth no man, but hath
committed all judgment unto the Son.*

John 5:22

Judgment

God's relatively simple standard of judgment—how well we obey His commandments
once we have learned them—was corrupted
during the Great Apostasy and had to be restored in the latter days.

When God the Father presented the plan of salvation to
His spirit children at the premortal council in heaven, He
not only outlined its purpose but laid out the standard
by which all mankind would be judged: "And we will
prove them herewith," He declared, "to see if they will do
all things whatsoever the Lord their God shall command
them."[1] This standard is relatively simple: we must learn
what God tells us to do and then do it!

This doctrine of judgment—based on mankind's
knowledge and obedience—was corrupted during the Great
Apostasy. By Joseph's time, most Christian churches taught
that when men and women accepted and confessed Jesus as
their personal Savior, their salvation was assured—which
essentially eliminated any potential consequences for their

---

1   Abraham 3:25.

actions. This teaching differed sharply from God's requirements and mandated that a restoration of His original doctrine take place.

God's judgment of mankind's obedience to His commandments has always existed. However, while denizens of the earth can claim that they successfully followed the Lord's plan in the pre-existence (based on the fact that they were born into mortality—a gift denied those who followed the devil), His judgment of their thoughts and actions while in mortality will have eternal consequences.

God's Judgment in the Pre-existence

Judgment began early for mankind. After being educated by God in the pre-existence and seeing Lucifer rebel against the Father's plan, men and women arrived at a point in their progression where they were required to choose whom they would follow: God or Satan. The plan of salvation required them to follow God, but they were free to make their own choice. However, once they exercised that choice a judgment came into play: those who chose to follow God would continue on to a temporal existence under the plan of salvation; those who chose to follow Satan would not.[2] The followers of Satan became subject to an irrevocable judgment that prohibited them from coming to earth to receive a physical body. They were doomed to eventually reside in outer darkness, a kingdom devoid of the Father's glory and therefore a place of "everlasting . . . endless . . . [and] . . . eternal punishment." A place where the "worm dieth not, and the fire is not quenched, . . . [and] the end, the width, the height, the depth, and the misery thereof" cannot be understood by any except those who find themselves under this condemnation.[3]

A partial judgment also appears to have been exercised

> Judgment began early for mankind.

---

2   Revelation 12: 7-9.

3   D&C 76:43-49; see also D&C 76:25-39; Abraham 3:22-28.

upon some of those who accepted God's plan while they were yet in their preexistent state, as evidenced by the following experiences of Abraham and Jeremiah.

After Abraham came to earth, he received a personal revelation wherein he spoke with God "face to face."[4] It was during this revelation that God made a solemn covenant with him, known as the Abrahamic covenant. God showed Abraham in vision many preexistent spirits and told him that some of those spirits had been chosen to be leaders on the earth because they had been "noble and great" in their premortal existence. God informed Abraham that he was one of these noble and great spirits and that he had been chosen before he was born.[5]

Jeremiah was also told about his preexistent status. The scriptures indicate that the Lord knew him before he was born, and had sanctified and ordained him to be a prophet to the nations.[6] It is reasonable to assume that all great prophets are so distinguished. Joseph Smith seemed to affirm this when he declared that all who were called to minister to the people of the world were designated to receive such a call *before the world was.*[7]

> Some were chosen in the pre-existence to be leaders.

This evidence leads us to the conclusion that some type of judgment in the pre-existence could have affected our earthly circumstances. It should be remembered, however, that the extent of this judgment was left behind the veil at birth. In most instances, we can only speculate as to whether there is a relationship between our mortal circumstances and what we did in the pre-existence.

Man's Judgment on Earth

As stated in the introduction to this chapter, most Christian churches teach that men are not saved by works,

---

4   Abraham 3:11.

5   Abraham 3:22–23.

6   Jeremiah 1:5.

7   TPJS 365.

but by their faith alone. But truths brought forth in the Restoration—such as our knowledge of the pre-existence—along with numerous scriptures from the Bible, provide us with a proper understanding of what God expects of us. That we are, in fact, responsible for our actions and our thoughts while in this life.

We all make judgments. This is one way we determine our relationship with God and our fellow man. When we are children, parents and other adults exercise judgment over us regarding our food, clothing, friends, recreation, education, and religion. "Train up a child in the way he should go," the scripture says, "and when he is old, he will not depart from it."[8] When we progress to adulthood, we start making our own judgments. Our judgments may not always be sound, however, and the wisdom so simply expressed in Proverbs is often lost in the results of our actions. Nonetheless, God will ultimately judge our choices in this life by the same standard He used to judge our premortal choices—by the degree of our obedience.

> Wisdom acquired in youth is often lost in the results of our actions.

Unfortunately, mankind often complicates this simple concept and thereby loses the true doctrine. For example, the Jews at the time of Christ were trained to regard different types of suffering as necessary or consequential to a corresponding sin.

> ... [U]p to thirteen years of age a child was considered, as it were, part of his father, and as suffering for his [father's] guilt. More than that, the thoughts of a mother might affect the moral state of her unborn offspring, and the terrible apostasy of one of the greatest Rabbis, had, in popular belief, been caused by the sinful delight his mother had taken

---

8   Proverbs 22:6.

when passing through an idol-grove. Lastly, certain special sins in the parents would result in specific diseases in their offspring, and one is mentioned as causing blindness in the children.[9]

These ancient Jews also taught the following relationship between worldly riches and righteousness: "The good man, if prosperous, [is] so as the son of a righteous man; while the unfortunate good man [suffers] as the son of a sinful parent. So, also, the wicked man might be prosperous, if the son of a goodly parent; but if unfortunate, it [shows] that his parents had been sinners."[10]

> There is no correlation between wealth and righteousness, and poverty and unrighteousness.

The Savior disavowed this automatic cause and effect relationship when He healed a man who had been blind from birth.[11] When questioned as to who had sinned, the man or his parents, thus causing the man to be born blind, Jesus replied, "Neither hath this man sinned, nor his parents." Then He explained that the man had been born blind so that the works of God could be manifest.[12]

On another occasion, some people told the Savior about some Galileans whose blood had been mingled with Pilate's sacrifices. Jesus replied, "Suppose ye that these Galileans were sinners above all the Galileans, because they suffered such things? I tell you, Nay." He also made it clear that the eighteen men who were killed by a tower that fell on them in Siloam had not died because of sin. They had simply been in the wrong place at the wrong time.[13]

It was man who developed the *sin-disease-punishment /obey-success-blessing* formulas—not God! While we should

---

9   Ed 2:178-179.

10   Geikie 2:298.

11   John 9.

12   John 9:1-3; Miracles 73.

13   Luke 13:1-5.

give thanks to God for all our blessings, material or otherwise, we do not necessarily receive worldly wealth and health because of our righteousness. Nor are we necessarily poor, unhealthy, or accident-prone because of our unrighteousness. It is sometimes difficult to determine if we are receiving a blessing or a punishment from God for any given thought or action, or just living with the results of a wise or an unwise choice. After all, it was the widow in her poverty who gave two mites and was judged by the Lord to be righteous, not the wealthy man who only gave of his abundance—yet they both gave.[14]

Isaiah 28:20 states, "For the bed [representing sin] is shorter than that a man can stretch himself on it: and the covering narrower than that he can wrap himself in it." Isaiah is implying that we are not always qualified to determine our own state of righteousness, let alone the blessings we feel we deserve. We are especially unqualified to determine the state of righteousness of others, or to ascertain what blessings they should receive. It is sufficient to know that this life is a determining factor in our final judgment; that the judgment we receive will be based on our thoughts and our actions; and that God, through His Son Jesus Christ, will be our ultimate judge.

> God, through His Son Jesus Christ, will be our ultimate judge.

There is one potential circumstance where men or women can be judged worthy of exaltation or damnation while they are still upon this earth. The decision is predicated upon the degree of an individual's righteousness or wickedness, and is given only if their calling and election has been made sure while they are yet in the flesh. Joseph Smith said having one's calling and election made sure is "knowing that [an individual] is sealed up unto eternal life, by revelation and the spirit of prophecy, through the power of the Holy Priesthood."[15] He explained that *knowledge* was

---

14   Mark 12:42–44.
15   D&C 131:5.

the key to the acquisition of this blessing, and that it was "impossible for a man to be saved in ignorance."[16] On the other hand, John teaches us in Revelation that individuals can become so wicked that they, too, can advance the day of their judgment (a negative *calling and election* that makes their condemnation sure), thereby sealing themselves to the devil and his kingdom in outer darkness—a condemnation from which they cannot escape (Revelation 13:16–18; SC, Chapter 8). However, even though men and women are responsible for bringing judgment upon themselves through their thoughts and actions, only God will make the determination of whether or not to advance their judgment, either to salvation or damnation.

John the Revelator saw a vision of the future in which the small and great of mankind stood before the Lord. The "books were opened," even "the book of life," and it was from these books that the fate of mankind was determined.[17] Malachi said a "book of remembrance" was written before the Lord from which those who "feared the Lord, and . . . thought upon his name" were remembered.[18] This book motif was carried forward from the time of Adam[19] to the latter days when the Lord declared in the Doctrine and Covenants that "All they who are not found written in the book of remembrance shall find none inheritance in" the day of judgment.[20]

The scriptures tell us that as a person "thinketh in his heart, so is he."[21] Since God knows what is in our hearts and understands the reasons for our actions, it behooves us to ask by what standard He will judge us.

> Faith and good works are both required for exaltation.

---

16   D&C 131:6.
17   Revelation 20:12.
18   Malachi 3:16.
19   Moses 6:5–8.
20   D&C 85:9.
21   Proverbs 23:7.

Once we learn His commandments, however, we realize that they form one of the standards by which we will be judged. If we have developed faith in God, we will *want* to obey Him. However, obedience requires action and action implies work, for as James notes, "faith without works is dead."[22] Why? Because *it is by our good works that our faith is demonstrated.* Still, neither *faith* nor *good works*, the one independent of the other, will get us to heaven. It requires a harmonious combination of the two.

Faith is the term used throughout the scriptures to characterize the degree of commitment we have to God. It is another standard by which the Lord will judge us and is the factor that motivates us to do His work. Early in the Restoration, the Lord testified that at the day of judgment He would "come to recompense unto every man according to his work, and measure to every man according to the measure which he has measured to his fellow man."[23] *Recompense* is an interesting word (especially considering the Lord's two great commandments). It means to give compensation for or to repay or reward. Therefore, we are going to receive compensation in kind for our work as a result of two things:

Our love of God
Fulfilling the First Great Commandment. This work is objective; our obedience to the commandments is defined. If we love God, we will not put anything before Him and His commandments. Our obedience to the first great commandment is therefore measured by the work we do in His behalf.

> We will be judged on how we live the First and Second Great Commandments.

Our love for our neighbors
Fulfilling the Second Great Commandment. This work

---

22   James 2:26.
23   D&C 1:10.

is subjective, undefined, and without limits. It measures how we treat our fellow man. The Lord gave the following example of how to live the second great commandment, but He coupled it with a warning:

> Then shall the King say unto them on his right hand, Come, ye blessed of my Father, inherit the kingdom prepared for you from the foundation of the world:
>
> For I was an hungered, and ye gave me meat: I was thirsty, and ye gave me drink: I was a stranger, and ye took me in:
>
> Naked, and ye clothed me: I was sick, and ye visited me: I was in prison, and ye came unto me.
>
> Then shall the righteous answer him, saying, Lord, when saw we thee an hungered, and fed thee? or thirsty, and gave thee drink?
>
> When saw we thee a stranger, and took thee in? or naked, and clothed thee?
>
> Or when saw we thee sick, or in prison, and came unto thee?
>
> And the King shall answer and say unto them, Verily I say unto you, Inasmuch as ye have done it unto one of the least of these my brethren, ye have done it unto me.
>
> Then shall he say also unto them on the left hand, Depart from me, ye cursed, into everlasting fire, prepared for the devil and his angels:
>
> For I was an hungered, and ye gave me no meat: I was thirsty, and ye gave me no drink:
>
> I was a stranger, and ye took me not in:

naked, and ye clothed me not: sick, and in prison, and ye visited me not.

Then shall they also answer him, saying, Lord, when saw we thee an hungered, or athirst, or a stranger, or naked, or sick, or in prison, and did not minister unto thee?

Then shall he answer them, saying, Verily I say unto you, Inasmuch as ye did it not to one of the least of these, ye did it not to me.

And these shall go away into everlasting punishment: but the righteous into life eternal.[24]

Once we understand the Lord's commandments, we become responsible for our actions. We will reap as we have sown[25] and be repaid according to our deeds.[26] If our works have been righteous, we will reap exaltation. But if they have been evil, we will reap "the damnation of [our] souls."[27] As Alma succinctly puts it: "[I]t is requisite with the justice of God that men should be judged according to their works; and if their works were good in this life, and the desires of their hearts were good, that they should also, at the last day, be restored unto that which is good. And if their works are evil they shall be restored unto them for evil."[28]

As one who has the ability to observe and understand our daily thoughts and actions, the Lord will understandably have no difficulty at the bar of judgment.

Judgment After Death

When we die, a judgment comes into play that allows

---

24   Matthew 25:34-46; Sermons 145.
25   Galatians 6:7-9.
26   Isaiah 59:18.
27   Alma 9:28.
28   Alma 41:3-4.

our spirits to move on to either the paradise of God or to a spirit prison. The factor that determines which condition our spirits will experience is our earthly righteousness and the knowledge we gained while in our probationary state.

The people of the world were judged by God prior to the Flood and were found sorely wanting. As a result, | A partial judgment will occur when we die.

the righteous who lived during the time of Enoch were taken into heaven by the Lord. Centuries passed, and during those decades many people made their calling and election sure and were taken into Enoch's city to await the resurrection. By the time of Noah, however, only eight righteous men and women were left upon the earth—Noah and his family. Noah had warned the people of God's impending judgment. He had told them about the devastating flood that would come upon them if they did not repent. But they would not listen. Consequently, Noah built an Ark, the waters rose, and only "eight souls were saved" alive.[29] Everyone else—men, women, and children—perished.

The wicked who lived during the centuries prior to Jesus Christ (including those who died in the flood) went to the spirit prison to await the mercies of God. Peter relates that following the Savior's crucifixion, He arranged for the gospel to be preached to those spirits "which sometime were disobedient, when once the long suffering of God waited in the days of Noah." Section 138 of the Doctrine and Covenants expands this number to include *all* disobedient spirits who reside, or will reside, in the spirit prison, and gives us further insight into how this missionary work is to be carried out.[30]

Judgment at the Second Coming
Whereas the wicked of Noah's time drowned in a uni-

---

29   1 Peter 3:20.
30   1 Peter 3:18-20.

versal flood, the wicked living on the Western Hemisphere in the meridian of time died in the massive destruction that occurred when the Savior of the world was crucified. Prophecy tells us that those who become wicked in the latter days (those unable to abide the Lord's presence) will be destroyed in the devastation that is prophesied to occur prior to the Lord's Second Coming. In addition to these cataclysmic destructions of the wicked, all who die in their sins without repentance, as well as those who die in ignorance of the gospel, will proceed to the "spirit prison" to await further knowledge which, when received, will give them the opportunity for exaltation.

At His advent, the Savior will come "with ten thousands of his saints, to execute judgment upon all

Missionaries will be sent to the spirits in prison.

. . . that are ungodly."[31] As portrayed in the parable of the wheat and tares, He will purge the earth, gather the righteous, and destroy the wicked.[32] John's vision of the Second Coming indicates that "one . . . like unto the son of man" will be instructed to "Thrust in thy sickle, and reap: for the time is come for thee to reap; for the harvest of the earth is ripe." And the one like unto the son of man "thrust in his sickle on the earth; and the earth was reaped."[33]

Judgment at the Second Coming will complete the two great harvests of the righteous. The first harvest took place at Jesus' resurrection, when all the righteous who had died prior to His time were themselves resurrected. This resurrection is considered *part* of the first resurrection, and is the "first" resurrection Alma looked forward to in Alma 40:16. All the righteous who have died (or will die) since Christ's resurrection, with the exception of those few men who had work to do during the Restoration, will remain in the grave until the general resurrection of the just at the

---

31 Jude 1:14–15.

32 Matthew 13:24–30; Parables 30.

33 Revelation 14:13–16.

Lord's Second Coming. This is the resurrection we commonly refer to as the "first" resurrection. These two resurrections reflect major judgments that have taken place, judgments that separate the righteous from the wicked. The wicked will be destroyed temporally to await a later resurrection, and the righteous will be resurrected when the Lord comes.[34]

The dead who are worthy to be resurrected at the Second Coming and the righteous men and women who are still living upon the earth at that time will be caught up to meet the Messiah at His glorious advent. However, those righteous individuals still in mortality will not be resurrected at that point. If they were, there would be no righteous men or women left upon the earth to carry on the Lord's work during the Millennium. They (and other worthy individuals who will be born during the Millennium) will be automatically resurrected when they reach "the age of a tree." They will then be caught up to the Lord's kingdom and their "rest shall be glorious."[35]

When the Lord comes again, many conditions will change. He will "bring to light the hidden things of darkness, and will make manifest the counsels of the hearts."[36] Isaiah further describes what life will be like during the millennium: "The vile person shall be no more called liberal, nor the churl said to be bountiful. For the vile person will speak villainy, and his heart will work iniquity, to practise hypocrisy, and to utter error against the Lord, to make empty the soul of the hungry, and he will cause the drink of the thirsty to fail."[37]

---

34 All men and women—good, bad, or indifferent—will eventually be resurrected. The revelation recorded in Section 88 of the Doctrine and Covenants provides us with more understanding of that process: "And the spirit and the body are the soul of man. And the resurrection from the dead is the redemption of the soul. And the redemption of the soul is through him that quickeneth all things, in whose bosom it is decreed that the poor and the meek of the earth shall inherit it" (D&C 88:14-17).

35 D&C 101:30-31.

36 1 Corinthians 4:5.

37 Isaiah 32:5-6.

* * *

The resurrection of Jesus Christ provides all mankind with the opportunity to live again—no strings attached. But the revelations and visions Joseph Smith received changed mankind's knowledge of the requirements for exaltation in God's kingdom. No longer would there be predestined individuals or groups who would automatically be privileged to live with the Father through no effort of their own, nor would there be arbitrary selection based on instantaneous acceptance of the Lord by those who perchance learned of Him and confessed Him without having complied with His commandments. Rather, there would be universal judgment based on the knowledge, faith, works, obedience, repentance, and accountability of each man and woman seeking His blessings. Thus, as the restored gospel teaches us, only through individual effort, the Savior's atonement, and ultimately the grace of God, will mankind be eligible for exaltation in the Father's kingdom.[38]

> The resurrection of Jesus Christ provided all mankind with the opportunity to live again.

> The Savior's atonement made it possible for us to repent of our sins.

We come from a loving Father who is always willing to forgive those who repent of their sins. In spite of this fact, we all have a tendency to be hard on ourselves when we evaluate our lives and the eternal disposition of our souls. But as John said, "if our heart condemn us," know that "God is greater than our heart, and knoweth all things."[39] We can place our confidence and trust in the Lord because all His judgments will be knowledgeable, merciful, and just.

38　Articles of Faith 1:3; 2 Nephi 25:23.

39　1 John 3:20.

PROSELYTING HELPS

God sent men and women to earth to prove them and see if they would do all things they were commanded to do. They will be judged by their thoughts and actions while in mortality. Although this simple standard of judgment was corrupted during the Great Apostasy, it was restored to the earth during the Restoration.

- When the Father's spirit children decided whose plan they would follow while in the pre-existence, a judgment came into play: those who followed the Father came to this earth and were blessed with a body, salvation (resurrection), and the opportunity for exaltation (living in God's kingdom); those who followed Satan were cast out of the Father's presence and will never receive any of these blessings.

- In vision, God showed Abraham many preexistent spirits who were noble and great individuals, and told him that some of those spirits had been chosen to be leaders on earth. This information intimates that our preexistent status could have an effect on our earthly circumstances.

- We make judgments as adults that may not be sound. The wisdom so simply expressed in Proverbs 22:6 is often lost in the results of our actions. In the end, God will judge us by the degree of our obedience, as he did in the pre-existence.

- It was man who developed the sin-disease-punishment / obey-success-blessing formulas, not God.

- Knowledge is an important element of salvation. We cannot be saved in ignorance.

- We are unqualified to determine the state of righteousness or unrighteousness of others. God, through His Son Jesus Christ, will be our ultimate judge.

- We are commanded to love God and to love our neighbor as ourselves: the First and Second Great Commandments.

- A partial judgment will occur when we die. We will either go to paradise or to the spirit prison—depending on how we've lived our lives. Missionaries will be sent to the spirits in prison to give them an opportunity to accept or reject the gospel.

- The resurrection of Jesus Christ provided all men and women with the opportunity to live again—no strings attached. The atonement of Jesus Christ made it possible for them to repent and be forgiven of their sins and through obedience, become candidates for exaltation.

- The restored gospel of Jesus Christ teaches us that universal judgment will be based on the knowledge, faith, works, obedience, repentance, and accountability of each man and women. Only through individual effort, the Savior's atonement, and ultimately the grace of God, will mankind will be eligible for exaltation in the Father's kingdom.

The final judgment is just that—final! Now is the time for men and women to prepare to meet their Maker. As member missionaries, we need to help others realize that they cannot wait to repent. The fullness of the gospel of Jesus Christ teaches that we will be judged by our thoughts and our actions. We can use the numerous scriptures from the Bible to help others realize that "faith without works is dead," that true faith leads us to good works, by which we perfect our lives and prepare to stand before the Lord.

In my father's house are many man-
sions: if it were not so, I would have told
you. I go to prepare a place for you.

John 14:2

The Kingdoms of Glory

Through information received during the restoration of the gospel, we know that resurrected beings will inherit different kingdoms
of glory depending on their obedience and
valiance during mortality.

Sometime during the Last Supper, the Lord said to His
Apostles, "In my Father's house are many mansions; if it
were not so, I would have told you. I go to prepare a place
for you."[1] But Jesus was not talking about actual buildings,
He was describing the kingdoms of glory that His beloved
Apostles could hope to attain in the hereafter.

Later, after the Lord's crucifixion, Paul was called as
an Apostle. As his ministry progressed, he wrote an epistle
to the Corinthians describing some of the different degrees
of glory that resurrected individuals could inherit based
on their valiance and obedience in mortality. He said,
"There are . . . celestial bodies, and bodies terrestrial: but
the glory of the *celestial* is one, and the glory of the *terrestrial*

---

1   John 14:2.

is another."[2] Although he only mentioned two glories in this verse, in the next verse he compared the glory of these bodies to the sun, the moon, and the stars[3] and in a later epistle, he testified that he had been "caught up to the third heaven"[4]—which implied that there was a third category which he had either failed to list or which was lost during transcription or translation. This category has subsequently been identified in the Doctrine and Covenants as a *telestial* body, which compares to the stars in its glory.[5]

In Joseph Smith's day, religious dogma generally held that there were only two places people could inherit in the hereafter: heaven or hell.[6] But the restored gospel indicated something quite different. While translating the Gospel of John, particularly John 5:29, Joseph Smith recorded the following in his journal:

> Four destinations exist for resurrected beings after the final judgment.

> Upon my return from Amherst conference, I resumed the translation of the Scriptures. From sundry revelations which had been received, it was apparent that many important points touching the salvation of man, had been taken from the Bible, or lost before it was compiled. It appeared self-evident from what truths were left, that if God rewarded everyone according to the deeds done in the body the term "Heaven," as intended

---

2   1 Corinthians 15:40. Emphasis added.

3   1 Corinthians 15:41.

4   2 Corinthians 12:2.

5   D&C 76:81.

6   The Christian belief in only heaven or hell could easily be viewed as a case of incomplete or corrupted knowledge since the plan of salvation also includes two interim conditions prior to the resurrection: paradise and the spirit prison. We all pass through one or the other prior to the final judgment. These states of existence could correlate to the Christian concept of heaven and hell, and may reflect the fact that knowledge of the kingdoms of glory had been lost or corrupted by recorded history.

220

for the Saints' eternal home must include more kingdoms than one.[7]

On February 16, 1832, Joseph and Sidney Rigdon (who was scribing for Joseph at the time) received the vision of the degrees of glory found in Section 76 of the Doctrine and Covenants. Joseph stated that both he and Sidney were in the Spirit when the vision was received and that "By the power of the Spirit our eyes were opened and our understandings were enlightened, so as to see and understand the things of God."[8] Perhaps no vision or revelation is attested to more often than this one as being received under the influence of the Spirit since several times throughout the revelation, the Lord commanded them to "write while . . . yet in the Spirit."[9]

In the revelation, Joseph and Sidney received information concerning the results of God's judgment, as well as detailed descriptions of who qualified for the various kingdoms. (They were also given other information that they were commanded *not* to write while "yet in the Spirit," because the information was "not lawful for man to utter.")[10] Following is a synopsis of what they recorded.

Outer Darkness

Several scriptures in Matthew symbolically describe outer darkness as a place where there is "weeping, and wailing, and gnashing of teeth."[11] This is the place where the sons of perdition and the devil and his angels will finally reside. There will be no glory in this kingdom.[12] Its inhabitants will not be visited by the Father or the Son or

---

7   HC 1:245.

8   D&C 76:12.

9   The Apostle John was also commanded to write while he was in the Spirit
     when he received the vision contained in the book of Revelation (Revelation
     1:10, 19).

10   D&C 76:113, 115.

11   Matthew 8:12; 22:13; 25:30.

12   D&C 76:25-39, 43-49.

the Holy Ghost. The men and women who go there will not be "redeemed in the due time of the Lord," but will come forth after all others have received their glory and been resurrected. They will be the last to come forth out of the grave, and will "reign with the devil and his angels in eternity." The "end thereof, neither the place thereof, nor their torment, no man knows," except those who are "partakers thereof." Its inhabitants will be those individuals whose sins are beyond the redemptive power of the Atonement.

Celestial Glory

After the sobering description of outer darkness, the vision next focuses on the opposite end of the spectrum and describes what Paul calls the "resurrection of the just" (or as John describes it, the "resurrection of life").[13] These are those who quality for the celestial kingdom.[14] The recipients of this kingdom will inherit a Celestial Glory. They are the men and women who "received the testimony of Jesus," kept the commandments, and were "sealed by the Holy Spirit of promise." They will become "gods, even the sons of God," and will come forth in the first resurrection to "dwell in the presence of God and his Christ forever and ever."[15] Paul, who undoubtedly either had a similar vision or knew of the doctrine by some other means, also declared that the individuals who inherit this kingdom will be those whose bodies are celestial, a glory he compared to the brilliance of the sun."[16] They will possess this kingdom forever and ever, "for, for this intent was it made and created, and for this intent are they [who inherit it] sanctified."[17]

---

13   John 5:29.

14   Acts 24:15.

15   1 Corinthians 15:40–41

16   D&C 76:51–70, 92–95.

17   D&C 88:20.

Terrestrial Glory

This glory is described as differing from that of the celestial glory as the "moon differs from the sun in the firmament." The inhabitants of this kingdom will be those who "died without law . . . [and] . . . received not the testimony of Jesus in the flesh, but afterwards received it." This will be home to the "honorable men of the earth" who were "blinded by the craftiness of men." They are described in the revelation as those who were "not valiant in the testimony of Jesus."[18] They will not inherit the presence of the Father, but they will be visited by Jesus Christ.

Telestial Glory

The last kingdom discussed in the revelation is the telestial kingdom. The citizens of this kingdom will be those who would not receive "the gospel of Christ, neither the testimony of Jesus," nor will they participate in the everlasting covenant. The revelation describes them as liars, sorcerers, adulterers, whoremongers, and those who love to lie. "These are they who suffer the wrath of God on earth . . . who suffer the vengeance of eternal fire . . . [and] are cast down to hell." They will be "as innumerable as the stars in the firmament of heaven, or as the sand upon the seashore." Although they will be visited by the Holy Ghost, they are still classified in the scriptures as those who will be "thrust down to hell." They will come forth in the last resurrection and the kingdom they inherit will differ in glory as the stars differ from the moon. Still, they are described as "heirs of salvation" in the revelation and when Joseph described their kingdom—the lowest of the glories of the Father—he said its beauty surpassed all understanding.[19]

The description of the kingdoms of glory that Joseph

---

18   D&C 76:71-80.

19   D&C 76:81-89; 99-109.

Smith received in vision differed sharply from the doctrine of the afterlife prevalent at his time (as it does today). It eliminated the ease by which mankind could attain God's presence and clearly defined what individuals must do if they want to inherit the Father's kingdom. Under the restored gospel, men and women will be judged by their faith *and* their works. James made this clear when he said, "Be ye doers of the word, and not hearers only, deceiving your own selves."[20] Therefore, in order to reach the highest of God's kingdoms we must have a firm, knowledgeable testimony that Jesus is the Christ; we must repent of all our sins; we must live all His commandments; we must be valiant in His cause; and we must endure faithfully to the end.

PROSELYTING HELPS

Based on information received during the Restoration, our state of righteousness during mortality will determine which kingdom we inherit.

- Four destinations are available to resurrected beings after the final judgment: the celestial kingdom, the terrestrial kingdom, the telestial kingdom, and outer darkness. The celestial is the highest kingdom and compares to the glory of the sun. The terrestrial compares to the glory of the moon and the telestial compares to the glory of the stars. Outer darkness, however, contains no glory at all and is symbolically described as a place of weeping, wailing, and gnashing of teeth.

- Those who received the testimony of Jesus, kept the commandments, and were sealed by the Holy Spirit of

---

20　James 1:22.

promise during mortality will inhabit the celestial kingdom. This is the kingdom where the Father dwells.

- Those honorable men and women of the earth who die without law or who were not valiant in the testimony of Jesus and were blinded by the craftiness of men will receive the terrestrial glory. Jesus Christ will visit this kingdom.

- The telestial kingdom will be inhabited by liars, sorcerers, adulterers, and whoremongers, those whom the scriptures say will be thrust down to hell. Still, Joseph Smith said the beauty of this low kingdom will surpass all understanding and that the Holy Ghost will be available to its inhabitants.

- The devil and his angels, together with those who commit unpardonable sins, will go to outer darkness—a kingdom without any glory at all. None of the Godhead will visit them. There will be "weeping, wailing, and gnashing of teeth" in this kingdom and only those who go there will know the depth of its torment.

- The restored gospel teaches us that no one automatically gets into heaven. Men and women will earn the kingdom they receive through the faith they exercise and the works they do.

The description of the kingdoms of glory Joseph Smith received in vision during the Restoration differs sharply from the doctrines of the afterlife other Christian religions teach, yet much of this information can be gleaned from the writings of the Apostles in the New Testament. The return of this information in the latter days is another evidence of the truthfulness of the Restoration.

SECTION VI

Final Evidences

*And now, seeing ye know these things
and cannot deny them except ye shall lie,
therefore in this ye have sinned, for ye have
rejected all these things, notwithstanding
so many evidences which ye have received;
yea, even ye have received all things, both
things in heaven, and all things which are
in the earth, as a witness that they are true.*

Helaman 8:24

Four Final Evidences

The Lord governs through law. He is highly organized. Law governs the seasons, the
movement of the earth and the planets, and
all the cycles of life because His house is a
house of order. This same orderliness is evident in the reinstatement of His gospel in
the latter days.

Although the LDS doctrines and practices that were restored
during the Restoration differed from the religious teachings
of Joseph's day, they had their roots in the Bible—scripture
that was available to most religionists of the time. Many important evidences have been discussed in preceding chapters, but to conclude the *Unique Evidences of the Restoration,*
four final, defining items need to be mentioned.

All Things are Governed by Law

The Lord declared that "all kingdoms have a law given . . . [and] he who is not able to abide the law of a celestial kingdom cannot abide a celestial glory. And he who cannot abide the law of a terrestrial kingdom cannot abide a terrestrial glory. And he who cannot abide the law of a telestial kingdom cannot abide a telestial glory . . . [however,] the earth abideth the law of a celestial kingdom, for it filleth the measure of its creation, and transgresseth not the law."[1]

The Lord has given a law "unto all things, by which they move in their times and their seasons." Their courses are fixed, "even the courses of the heavens and the earth, which comprehend the earth and all the planets."[2] The Lord's penchant for law is understandable in light of Section 132 of the Doctrine and Covenants, wherein it states, "Behold, mine house is a house of order, saith the Lord God, and not a house of confusion."[3] Even the Lord's blessings are regulated by law, for "there is a law, irrevocably decreed in heaven before the foundations of this world, upon which all blessings are predicated—And when we obtain any blessing from God, it is by obedience to that law upon which it is predicated."[4]

> If we receive a blessing from God, it is by obedience to the law upon which it is predicated.

It is no surprise, therefore, that the Restoration proceeded in such an orderly fashion—line upon line, precept upon precept—until the fullness of the Lord's gospel had been given to the Saints and His Church had been organized for the final time prior to the Second Coming. No other church so closely follows the format of the Savior's early church, nor exhibits the cohesiveness and organiza-

---

1   D&C 88:22-25.

2   D&C 88:42-43; Genesis 1:14.

3   Isaiah 28:10; D&C 132:8.

4   D&C 130: 20-21.

tional rationale that governs The Church of Jesus Christ of Latter-day Saints today.

The Age of Accountability

When discussing the Flood that occurred at the time of Noah, Peter said "eight souls were saved" from

| Children become accountable at the age of eight. |

the water. He then stated that the age at which an individual could be baptized was a "like figure" to the number of people who survived the Flood.[5] This is the earliest age at which an individual can be baptized into the LDS Church today, and was the age set by the Lord during the Restoration when He revealed that baptism by immersion was required of everyone after they reached the age of accountability. Then, after stating that parents were responsible to teach their children the requirements of baptism, He stated that if they did not teach them by the time they were "eight years old," the sins of the children would fall upon the heads of the parents.[6]

The restoration of this information contradicts the belief that infants need to be baptized to cleanse them of what some religionists claim is the original sin of Adam. In the second article of faith, Joseph Smith said, "We believe that men will be punished for their own sins, and not for Adam's transgression."[7] This declaration adamantly refuted the original sin doctrine being taught by the churches of Joseph's (and our) day.

Translated Beings

One of the more unusual evidences of the Restoration is the doctrine of translation. Although information concerning those who have been translated is scarce, the doctrine is referred to in general terms many times in the Bible. It is

---

5   1 Peter 3:20-21.

6   D&C 18:42; 68:25.

7   Articles of Faith 1:2.

first mentioned in the Old Testament where Enoch and his city (the city of Zion) are discussed. After Genesis recites Enoch's genealogical lineage down to Jared (his father),[8] the next four verses state:

> And Enoch lived sixty and five years, and begat Methuselah:
> And Enoch walked with God after he begat Methuselah three hundred years, and begat sons and daughters:
> And all the days of Enoch were three hundred sixty and five years:
> And Enoch walked with God: and he was not; for God took him.[9]

These verses by themselves might not lead us to believe that Enoch was translated; however, Paul made Enoch's status clear in a letter to the Hebrews when he wrote, "By faith Enoch was translated that he should not see death; and was not found, because God had translated him: for before his translation he had this testimony, that he pleased God."[10]

More information about Enoch is revealed in Chapters 6–8 of Moses in the Pearl of Great Price, a book of scripture that was received during the Restoration. From this we learn that not only Enoch was translated, but the entire city of Zion was taken up with all of its inhabitants.[11] The scriptures further indicate that those righteous individuals who lived upon the earth between the time of Enoch and the Flood of Noah were also translated (caught up into Zion).[12]

Elijah is another Old Testament prophet who was trans-

---

8   Genesis 5:18.
9   Genesis 5:21–24.
10   Hebrews 11:5.
11   Moses 7:21.
12   Moses 7:27.

lated: "And it came to pass, as they still went on, and talked, that behold, there appeared a chariot of fire, and horses of fire, and parted them both asunder; and Elijah went up by a whirlwind into heaven."[13] This reference to translation is somewhat vague. However, Joseph Smith clarified Elijah's status when, after seeing a vision of the Savior, Moses, and Elias in the Kirtland Temple, he recorded the following: "After this vision had closed, another great and glorious vision burst upon us; for Elijah the prophet, *who was taken to heaven without tasting death,* stood before us. . . ."[14]

Moses was undoubtedly translated also, else he could not have appeared to the Savior with Elias[15] when the Savior was transfigured before Peter, James, and John;[16] however, the Old Testament merely states that the Lord *buried* him, and that ". . . no man knoweth of his sepulcher unto this day."[17] The Book of Mormon sheds additional light on the biblical description of Moses' translation when in Alma 45:19 it states that the "Lord took Moses unto himself."

The last example from the Bible is John the Beloved in the New Testament. His translation was referred to during the visit of the resurrected Christ on the shore of the Sea of Galilee. On that occasion He said to Peter, "If I will that he [John] tarry till I come, what is that to thee? follow thou me. Then went this saying abroad among the brethren, that that disciple should not die. . . ."[18] A confirmation of John's translation was given in the Book of Mormon when three of the Lord's Nephite disciples hesitated to make a request of Him. The Lord declared to them, "Behold, I know your thoughts, and ye have desired the thing which John, my beloved, who was with me in my ministry, before that I was

---

13 2 Kings 2:11.
14 D&C 110:13. Emphasis added.
15 Elias is the New Testament name for Elijah.
16 Mark 9:4.
17 Deuteronomy 34:6.
18 John 21:22-23.

lifted up by the Jews, desired of me."[19] Finally, Section 7 of the Doctrine and Covenants also confirms that the Lord gave John "power over death,"[20] so that he could live and bring souls unto Christ.

In his journal, Joseph Smith clarified what it meant to be translated:

> Many have supposed that the doctrine of translation was a doctrine whereby men were taken immediately into the presence of God, and into an eternal fullness, but this is a mistaken idea. . . . Translation obtains deliverance from the tortures and sufferings of the body, but their existence will prolong as to the labors and toils of the ministry, before they can enter into so great a rest and glory [speaking of the resurrection]. They are of the "terrestrial order" [in their present state] and [are] "ministering angels."[21]

Persecution

In his writings, Peter recounted several experiences of those who were suffering because of their righteousness. He concluded by stating, "For it is better, if the will of God be so, that ye suffer for well doing, than for evil doing."[22] Paul wrote, "Yea . . . all that will live godly in Christ Jesus shall suffer persecution."[23] Paul was a living example of this, as his following litany of persecutions demonstrates:

> Whenever the gospel is established, the adversary attempts to destroy it.

---

19   3 Nephi 28:4-6.
20   D&C 7:2.
21   HC 4:210.
22   1 Peter 3:13-17.
23   2 Timothy 3:12.

Of the Jews five times received I forty stripes save one.

Thrice was I beaten with rods, once was I stoned, thrice I suffered shipwreck, a night and a day I have been in the deep;

In journeyings often, in perils of waters, in perils of robbers, in perils by mine own countrymen, in perils by the heathen, in perils in the city, in perils in the wilderness, in perils in the sea, in perils among false brethren;

In weariness and painfulness, in watchings often, in hunger and thirst, in fastings often, in cold and nakedness. . . .

In Damascus the governor under Aretas the king kept the city of the Damascenes with a garrison, desirous to apprehend me:

And through a window in a basket was I let down by the wall, and escaped his hands.[24]

If we had accurate records of the Apostles' ministries after the Lord's Ascension, it is probable that most of them would have been subjected to like persecution, as were the prophets of the Old Testament. Elijah was hounded from place to place, threatened with death, and persecuted by Ahab and Jezebel. Jeremiah was persecuted by almost everyone, from the king down to the common people. Eventually he was cast into a pit-like dungeon where he ". . . sunk in the mire" and suffered greatly.[25]

It is the nature of those steeped in apostasy, ignorance, avarice, and the desire for power to reject, persecute, and revile the prophets and people of God. Even the Savior himself fought the opposition of both Satan and the peo-

---

24 2 Corinthians 11:24-33.
25 Jeremiah 38:6.

ple as He attempted to establish His church, to the extent that He stated to those who followed Him: "Blessed are ye, when men shall revile you, and persecute you, and shall say all manner of evil against you falsely, for my sake. Rejoice, and be exceedingly glad: for great is your reward in heaven: for so persecuted they the prophets which were before you."[26]

The Prophet Joseph Smith was no exception. He suffered almost continual persecution from the time of his first vision until his untimely death at the age of thirty-eight. One of the cruelest attacks he endured occurred while he was living in Hiram, Ohio. He and Emma had adopted the Murdock twins when John Murdock's wife died in childbirth. The small infants had been ill with the measles for some time, causing sleepless nights for Joseph and Emma. On the night of March 24, 1832, Joseph suggested that Emma take the twin that was least ill and retire to the bedroom of the house so she could rest. Joseph took the other twin and retired to the trundle bed in the living room. After he had been asleep for some time, he was suddenly awakened by Emma's scream of "Murder!" Gaining consciousness, he realized that he was being carried out the door by about a dozen men. They were holding him in the air by his legs and arms while others had him by the shirt, trousers, and hair. He freed one leg and kicked a mobber, causing the man to fall to the porch. Moments later, the mobber thrust his bloodied hand into Joseph's face and said in a harsh voice, "I'll fix ya." The mob again secured him, threatening to kill him if he attempted any further resistance. They took him into a nearby field, making sure he was suspended in the air at all times.

Joseph pled with the mob not to kill him as they argued among themselves. They finally decided not to take his life, but only to tar him. They stripped him of all his clothing except the shirt collar around his neck. One mobber fell on

---

26   Matthew 5:11-12.

him and scratched him like a "mad cat," exclaiming, "that's the way the Holy Ghost falls on folks." Another mobber called for "Simonds," which Joseph correctly presumed to be one Simonds Ryder, a man who had apostatized from the Church because the Prophet had spelled his name wrong in a letter calling him to preach the gospel.[27] Simonds was asked where the tar bucket was and after a short search, it was found.

Initially, the mob decided to swab Joseph's mouth with tar because of his vocal outbursts, but Joseph moved his head to avoid it. Cursing at this maneuver, they then pressed a "vial" of tar into his mouth, but it broke on his teeth. They then proceeded to tar his naked body and left him lying in a field.

Joseph removed some of the tar from his lips so that he could breathe more easily and when he was able to stand, he looked around and could see several lights. He moved toward them, eventually ending up at Father Johnson's house. Several wives of the men taken by the mob, including Emma, had gathered at Father Johnson's. When Joseph arrived, the light reflecting off the tar on his naked body made it look like he was bleeding, and Emma fainted. Joseph called for a blanket. Once he had covered himself he entered the Johnson home where his friends spent the night scrapping and removing the tar from his body. By morning, he was ready to be clothed again. Since it was the Sabbath, the members of the Church in Hiram gathered together for services. Joseph's flesh was all "scarified and defaced" as a result of the efforts to remove the tar from his body during the night, but in spite of his condition, he

---

27 At a later date, Joseph responded to Simonds' inflammatory articles against the Church with a resolution in the *Times and Seasons*, Volume 6 page 841, which read: "Resolved, That as a last passing notice to all our enemies and apostates, of all grades, from Simonds Rider [again misspelling his name: "Rider" instead of "Ryder"] down to John C. Bennett and Sidney Rigdon, inasmuch as their bowels and mouths are like Etna and Vesuvius, full of filth and fire consuming their vitals, that they vomit toward the northern ocean, and leave Nauvoo, to take breath and live awhile in peace."

"preached to the congregation as usual" and "in the afternoon of the same day baptized three individuals."

In his journal, Joseph was particular to note that among others, the following mobbers were present at the church meeting: "Simonds Ryder, a Campbellite preacher and leader of the mob; one McClentic, who had his hands in my hair; one Streeter, son of a Campbellite minister; and Felatiah Allen, Esq., who gave the mob a barrel of whiskey to raise their spirits."[28]

The persecution the early Church brethren endured is definitive evidence of the Restoration. The fullness of the gospel of Jesus Christ was being restored and the adversary was doing all within his power to prevent it, just as he did when Christ restored the gospel during His ministry in the meridian of time. The Saints suffered expulsion from Ohio, Missouri, and Illinois, and the indignities of rape, murder, loss of business and personal property, and carnage of every kind. But the apex of their persecution was the martyrdom of Joseph and Hyrum Smith in Carthage Jail, a heinous act that was followed less than two years later by the unconscionably cruel expulsion of the Saints from Nauvoo in the dead of winter.[29]

Even after the Church was established in the western Great Basin, the Federal Government—goaded on by evil individuals—continued to persecute the Saints with every legal means at its disposal. Although it focused on the restored doctrine and practice of polygamy, it became clear that its express intent was to destroy the Church once and for all.[30]

In Volume III of the *History of the Church* compiled by

28 HC 1:261-264. Renditions of the tarring story from a book by Lucy Mack Smith, *The History of Joseph Smith* (American Fork: Covenant Communications, Inc., 2000), 219.

29 It is interesting to note that at the time of his death, the Prophet Joseph Smith was the mayor of Nauvoo, Illinois, and running for President of the United States.

30 Polygamy 72-96.

B.H. Roberts, Brother Roberts lists five major reasons for the persecutions in Missouri alone:

1. The difference of character between the Saints and the old settlers.

2. The misrepresentation of the Saints' views on slavery, i.e., charging them with being abolitionists.

3. Political jealousy. The Saints were beginning to outnumber the natives of Missouri.

4. The pretext that the Saints were communicating with the Indians for the purpose of despoiling the Gentiles and taking possession of their lands.

5. The folly of the Saints in boasting that the Lord would give them possession of western Missouri as an inheritance in the immediate future.

Brother Roberts concluded his analysis, however, by stating that the real cause of persecution in Missouri was the devil. But then, the same could be said for any of the periods of persecution during the Joseph Smith era, as well as those that occasionally occur today. It is the influence of evil—whether in individuals, religions, the militia, or governments—that precipitates persecution, antagonism, hatred, and murderous intent toward leaders or members of the modern Church.

PROSELYTING HELPS

The Lord's kingdom is orderly and consistent. Things that occurred and doctrines that existed during the meridian of time have been repeated and reinstated during the Restoration. Had it been otherwise, the gospel would not be true. The Lord's consistency is an all-encompassing evidence of the Restoration.

- The blessings we receive from God are predicated upon obedience to His laws.

- The Lord established the age of accountability as eight. This is the earliest age at which an individual can be baptized into the LDS Church today, and was the age set by the Lord during the Restoration when He revealed that baptism by immersion was required of everyone when they reached the age of accountability.

- Many Old Testament prophets were translated. John the Beloved in the New Testament was translated, as were three of the Lord's Nephite disciples. The doctrine of translation is an unusual evidence of the Restoration since some of these translated individuals appeared to Joseph Smith to restore elements of the gospel.

- Persecution follows those who would do the Lord's work. This is one of the devil's tools in his attempt to thwart the spread of the gospel. Persecution followed Christ and His Apostles and disciples in the meridian of time just as it did the Latter-day Saints in the early days of the Church. This is another evidence of the validity of the Restoration.

The restoration of the gospel in the latter days is preparing the way for the Lord's Second Coming. Through the interpretation of Nebuchadnezzar's dream in the book of Daniel, it is prophesied that the gospel will roll forth and fill the whole earth—for the last time. This prophecy is being fulfilled today and is perhaps the strongest evidence of the Restoration. Recognizing each of these evidences can strengthen our own testimonies and give us means to help others understand the truthfulness of the gospel.

And it is the Spirit that beareth witness, because the Spirit is truth . . . and the truth abideth for ever and ever.

1 John 5:6
D&C 1:39

Conclusion

It is interesting to note that no church besides The Church of Jesus Christ of Latter-day Saints has ever adopted all of the aspects of the Restoration presented in this book. A few have accepted some principles or doctrines, but deny others. Even the churches that existed throughout the Dark Ages, including those that claimed continuity from the Savior, failed to adopt these principles, and in many cases either repudiated them or changed them until they were unrecognizable.

But this is not unique in religious history. The ancient Israelites corrupted the Law of Moses which the Lord had established to prepare them for the restoration of the higher law and to help them recognize their Messiah. They chose, instead, to cherish and expand the ritual it contained, and ignored the fact that the sacrifices they performed day after day in the temple at Jerusalem were in similitude of He who would make the ultimate sacrifice for mankind.

The problem of doctrine becoming corrupt even occurred during the lives of Christ's Apostles, and was especially apparent after their deaths. Apostasy was inevitable as a dearth of knowledge befell the people and the Dark Ages were ushered in. It wasn't until the Lord called Joseph Smith as the first prophet of the latter days that the gospel could be restored in its purity.

The history of the LDS Church is a history of revelation upon revelation that fulfilled prophecy upon prophecy. Nothing the Prophet restored stands alone without scriptural support. When antagonists or apostates of the Church objected to any element of the Restoration, it required that they concoct a new and often bazaar interpretation of the scriptures in order to make them fit their hypotheses. It is no wonder that the enemies of the Prophet decided that the only way they could destroy the Mormon Church was to kill its leader. But they failed, just as any attempt to destroy the gospel will fail. When John the Baptist restored the Aaronic Priesthood, he stated that it would "never be taken again from the earth, until the sons of Levi do offer again an offering unto the lord in righteousness."[1] There is a sense of permanence in this scripture, as there is in Daniel's vision wherein a stone (representing the gospel) smites the worldly man-image in Nebuchadnezzar's dream and becomes a "great mountain" that fills the whole earth.[2]

Just as the Old Testament is a mirror through which the New Testament can be viewed, the New Testament is a mirror through which the Restoration can be viewed. It is evident that Joseph did not just *make up* the ordinances, principles, Church organization, doctrines, and priesthood offices restored in this last dispensation of time; rather, the Lord carefully orchestrated the restoration process.

"Search the scriptures," the Lord said, "for in them ye think ye have eternal life: and they are they which testify of me."[3] In spite of this admonition, most of the people living in Christ's time missed Him. It is sobering to realize that this same admonition can be applied to us today. "Search the scriptures," for they testify not only of the principles

---

1   D&C 13.

2   Daniel 2:35.

3   John 5:39.

and doctrines that have been restored in these latter days, they continue to testify of God and of the divinity of His Son, Jesus Christ. We would be wise to keep this admonition foremost in our thoughts else we, too, might miss Him.

$\mathcal{K}$ey to $\mathcal{A}$bbreviations

Quotes from the standard works of The Church of Jesus Christ of Latter-day Saints—the Bible, the Book of Mormon, the Doctrine and Covenants, and the Pearl of Great Price—are abbreviated in the standard manner.

AC   Lucien Carr, *Missouri: A Bone of Contention: American Commonwealths* (Boston and New York: Haughton, Mifflin and Company, 1896).

CC   Will Durant, *Caesar and Christ: The Story of Civilization,* vol 3. (New York: Simon and Schuster, 1963).

CE   *New Catholic Encyclopedia,* Vol. IV. (Washington D.C.: The Catholic University of America, 1967).

CHCC   Thomas Bokenkotter, *A Concise History of the Catholic Church,* revised ed. (Garden City, New York: Image Books, 1979).

Cook   Lyndon W. Cook, *The Revelations of the Prophet Joseph Smith: A Historical and Biographical Commentary of the Mormon 'Doctrine and Covenants'* (Salt Lake City: Deseret Book Company, 1983).

Ed   Alfred Edersheim, *The Life and Times of Jesus the Messiah,* reprint ed. (Grand Rapids, Michigan: Wm. B. Eerdmans Publishing Company, 1981).

FM   Thomas L. Snead, *The Fight For Missouri* (New York: Charles Scribner's Sons, 1888).

Geikie Cunningham Geikie, *The Life and Words of Christ,* revised ed., 2 vols. (New York: D. Appleton and Company, 1891, 1894).

GM   Golda Meir, *My Life by Golda Meir,* First American Edition (New York: G.P. Putnam's Sons, 1975).

HC   Joseph Smith, Jr., *History of The Church of Jesus Christ of Latter-day Saints,* ed. B. H. Roberts, 7 vols. (Salt Lake City: The Church of Jesus Christ of Latter-day Saints, 1955).

JD   Brigham Young et al., *Journal of Discourses* (London: Published privately, 1855–1886).

Miracles E. Keith Howick, *The Miracles of Jesus the Messiah* (St. George, Utah: WindRiver Publishing, 2003).

Mission E. Keith Howick, *The Mission of Jesus the Messiah* (St. George, Utah: WindRiver Publishing, 2003).

Parables E. Keith Howick, *The Parables of Jesus the Messiah* (St. George, Utah: WindRiver Publishing, 2003).

Polygamy E. Keith Howick, *Polygamy: The Mormon Enigma* (Silverton, Idaho: WindRiver Publishing, 2007)

Prophets E. Keith Howick, *Prophets of the Old Testament* (Silverton, Idaho: WindRiver Publishing, 2005).

Roberts B. H. Roberts, *A Comprehensive History of The Church of Jesus Christ of Latter-day Saints,* 6 vols. (Provo, Utah: Brigham Young University Press, 1965).

SC   E. Keith Howick, *The Second Coming of Jesus the Messiah,* (St. George, Utah: WindRiver Publishing, 2003).

Sermons E. Keith Howick, *The Sermons of Jesus the Messiah* (St. George, Utah: WindRiver Publishing, 2003).

Smith's William Smith, LLD, *Smith's Bible Dictionary,* Rev. F.N. & M.A. Peloubet. (Nashville: Thomas Nelson, 1962).

TPJS *Teachings of the Prophet Joseph Smith,* selected and arranged by Joseph Fielding Smith, Jr. (Salt Lake City: Deseret Book Company, 1958).

Torah *The Torah: A Modern Commentary,* Edited by Gunther Plaut. (New York: Union of American Hebrew Congregations, 1981).

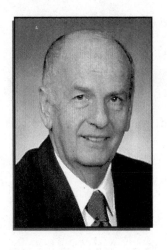

E. Keith Howick has a Master's degree in Political Science and a Juris Doctor degree in Law from the University of Utah. He has taught classes in American national government and graduate seminars in public law at Pennsylvania State University. He is a student of Mormon history and has given innumerable presentations discussing the history, people, and doctrine of the Church of Jesus Christ of Latter-day Saints including classes taught at the University of Utah, Brigham Young University, and Montana State University.

Keith and his wife Gail live in the historic Silver Valley of northern Idaho.